SUCCESSFUL HIRING FOR FINANCIAL PLANNERS

Best;
Caro

D0071774

ISBN: 0999510541
ISBN-13: 978-0999510544

For my father, who always told me he was proud of me.

CONTENTS

FOREWORD

O ne of the most ironic commonalities of today's experienced financial planners who have been practicing
for more than twenty years is that none of them actually
began their careers as financial planners. The reality was
that in the 1990s and prior, there were virtually no entry-
level jobs available for financial planners. In fact, the only
way to become a financial planner was to start out as a life
insurance agent selling insurance, or a stockbroker selling
stocks, bonds, or mutual funds, and if you were successful
enough at selling, then maybe after five to ten years you
might be allowed to pursue your CFP® Certification and
begin learning a financial planning process that went beyond just selling products.

In other words, the traditional career track for all of
today's experienced financial planners was that first they
earned (by prospecting and finding clients to sell products
to), and then they *learned* (to be a comprehensive financial planner and receive compensation for their advice).

Yet the great virtue of financial planning advice is that
it establishes an ongoing value to the advisor-client relationship beyond just what happens at the moment a product is sold, which, over the past twenty years, has support-
ed the growth of various types of recurring revenue business models, such as the AUM model. As a result, it has

become economically rewarding to deliver ongoing financial planning services to clients, beyond just leading up to the product sale, in order to retain their recurring revenue. In turn, this has led to both a demand for a growing volume of financial planners, and the opportunity for the more repetitive tasks of financial planning to be delegated to "junior" financial planners, which has driven the emergence of an entire career track from associate financial planner to lead financial planner to partner.

Fortunately, the rising demand for entry-level financial planning talent has been met, at least in part, by an explosion in undergraduate level college degree programs for financial planners. For example, in the past fifteen years, the number of degree-granting financial planning programs has more than doubled to over one hundred, of which nearly one-third are graduate degree or doctoral programs. And after a lull during the financial crisis of the late 2000s, the number of candidates sitting for the CFP® exam is currently at its highest point in over a decade, with record numbers of candidates in their twenties and thirties sitting for the test each year.

However, even with the booming growth of college programs for prospective CFP® professionals, and an ever-rising demand for young talent as more advisory firms adopt recurring revenue models that support additional hiring, most firms today seem to continue struggling to hire young talent. And prospective young financial planners often talk with disdain of the poor quality of financial planning jobs available to them.

In many cases, the generational gap is to blame, as today's new financial planners are typically millennials, while the founders are baby boomers. The differences between these generations, in everything from their communication style to their expectations of a work-life balance, has made hiring and retention a challenge for many advisory firms.

Yet, arguably, the real driver of this divide is something much more straightforward: At the moment most advisory firms hire an associate planner, it is the first time they've actually tried to hire a professional-track staff member (beyond administrative staff), and usually the first time they've had to formalize a professional career track in their firm, which is necessary to attract and retain top talent. Simply put, most firms have no experience in hiring a professional entry-level financial planner, and are just figuring it out as they go—and not always very well.

Even more fundamental is the fact that while every experienced financial planner today followed a career progression of "earn then learn," the reality is that today's new financial planners coming out of school have *already* learned more about financial planning than their bosses likely learned during the first decade of their careers. As a result, new financial planners are rejecting the traditional "earn then learn" approach, and want to see an opportunity to apply what they've learned first, and then grow to the point where they earn by sourcing their own clients. This means that experienced advisory firm owners can't just recreate the career path that they themselves followed, because the next generation expects and demands a different kind of career progression altogether.

Ultimately, it was these blocking points—the mismatched expectations of firm owners hiring new financial planners, and what the top new financial planners themselves were actually seeking—that led Caleb and I to create

New Planner Recruiting, and why I ultimately urged him to write down everything he's learned in more than a decade of dealing with these issues, which culminates in the book you're about to read.

From figuring out your hiring needs, to crafting an effective job description, identifying and vetting top talent, formulating an appealing career track, and making the right compensation offer, "Successful Hiring for Financial Planners" is meant to be a straightforward guide that is full of practical wisdom and real-world experience for how to effectively execute the hiring process for your first (or next) financial planner in your growing advisory firm.

In the end, financial planning is a service business, with human talent being the single greatest line item expense on a firm's profit and loss statement. Given that a single financial planner can only support a finite number of clients, the key to success and long-term growth in any advisory firm is the ability to attract and retain an ever-growing volume of top talent to serve an ever-growing base of clients. Very simply, a successful advisory firm needs successful advisors to succeed, and successful advisors need a successful advisory firm to have their own growth and career progression opportunities. The bottom line is *their success is your success*, and I hope this book supports your mutual success for years to come.

Michael E. Kitces, MSFS, MTAX, CFP®, CLU, ChFC
Co-Founder, New Planner Recruiting
Publisher, Nerd's Eye View
www.kitces.com

INTRODUCTION

This is a pivotal time for the financial planning profession. We're facing a talent shortage that is projected to continually worsen in the years to come. According to the Bureau of Labor Statistics, through 2024 the employment needs for personal financial advisors is expected to increase by 30 percent in North America. Furthermore, the Social Security Administration estimates that roughly 11,000 baby boomers are retiring every day! Unfortunately, only 7,000 potential financial advisors are taking the CFP® Certification Exam each year, which is woefully short of the number that is required to serve the growing population.

While these statistics demonstrate the tight talent market and severe shortage of financial planners that has been plaguing our profession for the last several years, they also present an opportunity, which is why I wrote this book. In the chapters ahead, I'll help business owners become substantially more prepared to tackle the talent shortage affecting our profession by teaching them how to effectively and efficiently staff their financial planning firms. My goal is to help these enterprises grow so they can serve the consumers who are in need of their guidance the most.

Assessing the Need for Financial Planners

While the future talent outlook for the profession may look grim, it's not helped by the fact that a growing number of financial planners are working exclusively with younger Generation X and Y clients, and are not serving the baby boomer generation at all. In total, there are some 76 million baby boomers alive today, along with 141 million consumers belonging to Gen X and Y. Combined, these produce a total population of 217 million consumers in the U.S. who are potentially in need of professional financial advice. If there are 323,000 active financial planners today, and an estimated 10,000 to 15,000 planners are retiring each year, that means that each active planner would have to service nearly 700 clients! Assuming that one financial planner can effectively advise about 100 clients depending on the service model, the need for financial planners is stronger than it's ever been.

Hiring Struggles Facing Financial Planning Firms

Hiring struggles in small businesses have been well documented, and recently released research from Leadership IQ does not paint a rosy picture. Instead, it highlights the fact that 46 percent of all new hires fail within 18 months. This is not a promising figure on the surface, but it requires further analysis. The top five reasons that new hires were not successful was because they:

1. lacked the ability to be coached;
2. were not able to understand their emotions, as well as those around them;
3. were not motivated to achieve their full potential;
4. lacked the proper temperament; and
5. lacked technical competence.

Fortunately, these five items can be easily identified and mitigated as a result of a thorough recruiting process. My experience has been that most business owners tend to place too much emphasis on technical competence because it is what they're familiar with and it's the easiest to measure. But a lack of technical competence only accounts for 11 percent of new hire failures, according to recent research. Instead of business owners assuming, "If they are technical, then I can teach them everything else," they should be thinking, "If they have motivation, emotional intelligence, appropriate temperament, and are coachable, then I can teach them the technical aspects later." Interpersonal skills are a better predictor of a new hire's impending success or failure, and this should encourage business owners to analyze the softer side of candidates whom they are considering. By focusing on each candidate's interpersonal skills during the interview and recruitment process, they will help ensure the future success of their new hire.

Make Hiring a Priority

Most firms tend to delay the hiring process until their busiest time of the year when they feel understaffed and overworked. The result is inadvertently beginning a labor-intensive recruiting process at the most inopportune time, when they are busy with year-end client work, software conversions, annual reporting, etc. To avoid this common mistake, strive to take on hiring projects at least three to six months before you anticipate needing additional staff, or when you reach 70 to 80 percent capacity. Also, consider initiating the hiring process during what are typically considered the slower summer months. But beware, if you're seeking a new college graduate, the cycle will need to begin much earlier in the year. Today, it's common to find the most talented students having a start date of June 1 after graduating in May.

Understanding the Talent Pool: Gen Y

Generation Y, sometimes referred to as millennials, Gen Text, and Gen Why, are those born between 1978 and 2000. While they undoubtedly possess a unique set of characteristics, these characteristics can sometimes leave others, mainly baby boomers, scratching their heads. Since most financial planning firms tend to be owned by baby boomers, and most new advisors tend to be from Gen Y, some intergenerational coaching may be helpful.

Here are some basic Gen Y tendencies that can frustrate firm owners, and the techniques that can be used to turn these potential pitfalls into advantages.

- **Tendency #1: Asking *why* a task has to be performed.** When Gen Y'rs ask why they have to perform a certain task, assuming it is framed in a non-threatening way, they're really asking how the specific task fits into the larger scope of the overall project. They want to know that they're making a difference and contributing to the greater good. As an employer, make sure that you show them how their contributions effect clients and how their efforts directly impact the product or service that you're offering. Explain this concept once and have them document it, so that you can use it as a future reference for all new hires.

- **Tendency #2: Ending the workday at 5 o'clock sharp.** Gen Y'rs disdain for logging long hours at the office or working weekends is likely a byproduct of their parents saying, "Don't work all the time like I did!" and "There's more to life than just work." From the Gen Y'rs perspective, work and leisure should never mix, and this group desperately wants to achieve a fulfilling work-life balance. As an employer, consider having flexibility regarding work hours, as long as your expectations are clear, the work is getting done, and employees are available to respond to client needs as they arise. Furthermore, consider offering rewards such as leaving early on certain days or taking additional time off as needed. These tend to be terrific motivators for this group. In fact, these perks tend to have an even bigger impact than financial rewards. Since Gen Y'rs are two generations removed from the Great Depression, they don't have the same drive to accumulate money and financial stability as their baby boomer bosses.

- **Tendency #3: Preferring electronic communication.** Technology is a large part of a Gen Y'rs life. Emailing, texting, Tweeting, and Instagramming are preferred channels of communication for this group. They were the first generation to grow up with email and instant messaging, so they are used to getting answers immediately, which allows them to move on to their next task and get closer to their coveted leisure time. As an employer, you should recognize that the preference for these new communication channels has thrust some Gen Y'rs into the workforce without fully allowing them to develop their interpersonal skills. Be aware of this and screen for it when hiring.

- **Tendency #4: Not willing to take criticism.** Many Gen Y'rs grew up overly sheltered and protected by their parents so they would not have to experience rejection. (Remember, everyone gets a blue ribbon!) Because many Gen Y'rs have never experienced rejection—and we all know that rejection is a way of life in the business world—employers should be cognizant of the frequency and dosage of criticism they offer. Do not refrain from giving constructive criticism, but remember to give positive feedback when it is due, as well.

Understanding the Talent Pool: iGen

The generation following Gen Y, known as "iGen," are those born around the turn of the millennium. These new kids on the block are teenagers poised to make a major impact in the workplace in the years to come. If you would like to add a candidate from iGen to your firm, perhaps as a summer intern, consider the following methods to source, screen, integrate, and retain them.

Sourcing—Campus visits and social media continue to be useful ways to locate and connect with this group of candidates. They prefer Instagram and Twitter over Facebook. They have also seen their older peers in Gen Y make mistakes by posting inappropriate items online, so they tend to be much more protective of their brand and online privacy—which is one of the reasons why Facebook is lower on their priority list.

Screening—This group is used to being able to find information quickly through various technological platforms. Instead of having them memorize facts and answer questions via traditional tests, give them exercises that require them to locate appropriate resources and use them to solve problems in a timely manner. As an employer, what's most important is assessing how they approach solving a problem, how quickly they're able to solve it, and the accuracy of their work. Rote memorization and regurgitation-type exercises are not the best measures to assess an iGen candidate's capabilities.

Integrating—The use of smartphones by iGen is even more prevalent than prior generations—hard to imagine, I know! Some even say it's acceptable to use smartphones during job interviews! As an employer, carefully review your policies and procedures surrounding technology to ensure they continue to align with your philosophies and the changing demographics of today's workforce. It's worth noting that only 6 percent of the respondents from a leading iGen survey thought that it was appropriate to talk, text, or surf the Web during business hours, compared to 18 percent of millennials. In other words, iGen employees are more connected to technology, but they may actually be better at respecting its boundaries than their millennial counterparts.

Retaining—iGen employees tend to need a technology-centric culture and continuous learning environment, which is not all that dissimilar from millennials. However, they're concerned more about online privacy than millennials, and social media determines their personal and professional satisfaction to a larger degree. This means that they could likely turn out to be more entrepreneurial, as they have witnessed firsthand the overnight successes of startups on social media. As an employer, be aware of this mindset and use it to your advantage to tactically position your firm for the future.

Moving forward, understand that if you cannot communicate in five or fewer words, and/or with a large picture, it will be difficult to attract and retain iGen employees. As the war for talent tightens, the firms targeting younger workers and building robust internship programs to develop their human capital pipeline will be best positioned for success.

The Outlook of the Financial Planning Industry

Despite the unique hiring challenges facing financial planning firms today, the future of the industry looks bright. Financial planning is frequently named as one of the fastest growing and most rewarding careers. In fact, "Financial Planner" was recently named the #6 best job in America by CNN Money and #5 by CareerCast.com. It's also worth noting that CNN Money listed "Financial Planner" as the #3 Best Job for Fast Growth. We should remind ourselves and our employees of this frequently.

Keep in mind, however, that hiring is cyclical and heavily dependent on the health of the financial markets. Currently, there are many firms looking for exceptional talent and this will inevitably slow down the next time the stock market corrects. With that in mind, candidates that are passionate for the profession, are coachable, have demonstrated initiative, and want to spend their careers serving others will continue to remain attractive, even during the downturns.

Developing consistent titles for a new planner's career path will also help develop the profession. The natural progression of an aspiring financial planner's career should be as follows: Financial planning student, financial planning intern, associate financial planner, lead financial planner, and then partner. Furthermore, if firms eventually want their newly hired financial planners to work directly with clients, referring to them as "Junior," "Support," and "Assistant" externally is not effectively positioning them to do so.

In the chapters that follow, I'll continue to help demystify the hiring process so that you can grow your business and increase your firm's efficiency and productivity. By first showing you how to determine your staffing needs, and then demonstrating how to successfully screen and onboard new hires, you'll be able to position your firm for unlimited success. And finally, by showing you how to integrate and retain your key personnel, you'll be able to strategically overcome future obstacles with ease and excitement.

CHAPTER 1

Determining Your Needs

When hiring new planners for associate planner positions, many firm owners ask me to find someone just like them. As the Peter Lynch saying goes, "Buy what you know." Owners tend to want to take the same approach when it comes to hiring. It's human nature after all—we prefer to stay in our comfort zone rather than venturing into the unknown.

However, I often find that firm owners have not thoroughly considered the position's required activities or the candidate's expectations before beginning the hiring process. As an owner, you should begin by having a good understanding of your firm's overall needs. For example, if your skill set is strategic visionary and primary relationship manager, then you should strive to find a candidate with a complementary skill set to fill in the gaps. Frankly, too much overlap in a small organization will lead to inefficiencies.

If you're a strategic thinker, you'll need to hire someone to implement your ideas and carry out your vision. Or, if you're gifted at bringing in new clients, you'll need someone to help serve your existing client base. At this stage of your career, you should have a strong idea of where your gifts and passions lie. Once that's been fully established, you should consider hiring someone to perform the tasks that you're not good at, or don't want to be doing, so that you can focus on your core competencies instead.

Here are a few questions that you should consider before attempting to hire a new employee. These questions will help determine role identification and job fit characteristics.

- What am I good at that I want to spend the majority of my time doing?
- How will this new hire fit in with our existing company culture?
- What tasks will he or she be able to do that I no longer want to?
- What is currently lacking in my client service and deliverable model?
- Do I want to teach a new hire the business of financial planning? Do I want to be a manager?
- Am I willing to take a temporary step back in both income and time, in order to take steps forward in the future?
- Do I want an ensemble, silo, or sole practitioner structure for my firm?

Spending the appropriate amount of time identifying your needs before blindly diving into the hiring process is necessary to finding a good long-term fit for your organization. I see a lot of mistakes occur when firm owners try to hire someone exactly like them, and place them in a support role indefinitely—a combination which is rarely successful.

Hire a New College Grad or Career Changer?

When a firm sets out to hire an associate financial planner, they will generally hire either a new college graduate with a degree in financial planning, or a career changer with a certificate in financial planning. The differences between a certificate and a degree program can be substantial, and should be carefully considered before deciding which type of candidate to pursue.

When deciding between these two types of candidates, consider the following advantages and challenges.

Advantages to Hiring a Career Changer

Newly hired financial planners that come from unrelated fields are likely to have strong professional backgrounds already, compared to new college graduates. In addition, they have inevitably had to make personal financial decisions over the years, so basic financial planning knowledge should already be present. From developing a household spending plan, to determining how to allocate funds in a 401(k), to possibly even reviewing estate documents, they likely aren't as inexperienced as you may assume. It's also possible that they've been through major life events, such as the birth of a child, death of a spouse, divorce, major job loss, or death of a parent. This kind of "real world experience" can be invaluable in making personal connections with clients and relating to their unique situations. Earlier in my career, when I was a young financial planner in my twenties, I remember a client telling me that he was divorcing his wife and he needed my guidance. I wanted to crawl under my desk because I didn't know what to say, and I definitely couldn't relate!

Advantages to Hiring a New College Graduate

While most new college graduates won't have the life experience that career changers possess, there are some that do, like candidates that served in the military, completed a mission of service through their church or nonprofit organization, or have parents who are small business owners. Another advantage of this group is that they tend to be much more flexible about relocating for the right job opportunity, even if it's across the country. This is because they're less likely to have family ties, concerns about employment for a spouse, or worries about the quality of the local school system at their young age. Furthermore, since they may not yet have family commitments, they can often get by on earning less income, which equates to a willingness to accept lower entry-level pay.

Challenges to Hiring a Career Changer

For career changers, their roles and responsibilities, career trajectory, and compensation can all be areas of potential conflict because of their career stage and income history. Those that are changing from careers where they were successful are often confused as to why they cannot immediately earn the same income as a financial planner. Others have realistic expectations about compensation, but can still be frustrated as to why they have to learn from the ground up. Their common sentiment is, "I shouldn't have to fill out that form or perform that task because in my prior career there was a team that did that for me." Alternatively, prior work experience with a different company may allow some career changers to more fully appreciate their new firm and what it has to offer.

Challenges to Hiring a New College Graduate

The transient nature of new college graduates has been a well-documented frustration of many employers. These grads are beginning their lives as adults, and sometimes it takes time to find the right career path. In prior generations, changing jobs was not a viable option because it meant giving up a job title, company car, and pension. But today, the younger workforce has a wide range of opportunities scrolling before them and fewer ties to their current employers. For example, a few years ago a firm that I work with had an employee abruptly resign after working for a year or two so that he and his spouse could travel the world for a year. He gave up a well-paying, stable job, and she gave up an even better paying job at a Silicon Valley tech giant. As a firm owner, recognize that just as your firm's wants and needs can change over time, so too can those of recent college grads. It's best to accept the fact that younger employees will have a greater tendency to change their careers in the months and years ahead.

For further insight, the following chart provides additional perspective that I've gained based on thousands of anecdotal conversations, decisions, and reactions with both groups in the workplace. My company, New Planner Recruiting, tends to place roughly the same amount of new college graduates and career changers over the course of a year. Although there will always be outliers, you should use this chart as a framework to determine who will be the best fit for your firm.

	New College Grad	Career Changer
Life Experience	Usually low	Mid to high
Financial Planning Experience	Some; Internships required for some degree programs	Some; Personal experience only
Existing Biases	Usually none, but increasing	Often substantial
Technology Skills	High to very high	Low to high
Relocation Flexibility	High	Low to mid
Income Requirements	Low to mid	Low to high

To Relocate or Not to Relocate

After deciding which type of new planner to hire, the next decision is whether to target local or remote candidates. For example, I'm often contacted by firm owners who believe they've found the perfect candidate, but they're concerned because she lives out of state with no ties to the area. They worry the candidate will relocate for the position, only to move back home a short while later if she's dissatisfied. When I'm presented with this scenario, I reiterate to business owners that they must always accept a certain degree of risk when hiring new employees, and that includes the risk of them leaving the firm once the training process has been completed. While it's true that the risk increases when hiring someone who does not have familial ties to the area, it's not necessarily an assurance of impending disaster.

A few items that you should consider in order to minimize the risks associated with relocating a new hire are:

Make Sure the Candidate Has Visited Your Area— A candidate who is familiar with your firm's city is more likely to understand the climate, culture, and cost of living. The importance of this basic understanding of the quality of life cannot be underestimated. For example, if a candidate tells me that he wants to live somewhere warm and then proceeds to list San Francisco as his top choice, it's likely not going to turn out well for him. You should insist that candidates familiarize themselves with the local area as a means of screening out those who will not be a good long-term fit.

Spend Time Getting to Know the Candidate—Give the candidate a tour of your office and plan for at least one outside-the-office activity. I also recommend sharing a few meals and possibly inviting the candidate to your home. This will make the candidate feel valued and will give you ample time to consider your hiring decision.

Have the Candidate Create a Budget—This is an exercise that I encourage all candidates to complete when seeking employment in large metropolitan areas. I find those who take the time to do this are much more serious about relocating, while those who don't are at risk of underestimating the cost of living and regretting their decision to relocate. Of course, it's also a worthwhile experience for financial planning career changers, as they'll likely be helping their own clients create budgets, too. The key point is to ensure that candidates don't face sticker shock if your firm is based in a notoriously expensive city.

Observe How the Candidate Handles the Interview Process—If a candidate insists that you fly him out for an interview, all expenses paid, he may not be as committed as you would like. This is more of a general entitlement and initial screening tool, but candidates who are willing to get in their cars and make an extra effort to come to your office for an interview and/or offer to share in the cost of travel, tend to be extremely strong candidates.

Use these tips to differentiate serious candidates who can add substantial value to your organization, from those who are just looking for you to finance their next great adventure. Keep in mind, however, that employees today don't necessarily set out with the expectation to stay with the same company for thirty years like prior generations. While it may not be ideal, it's realistic to expect a new hire to remain with your firm for five to ten years. Remember, the younger generation of talent doesn't measure success on tenure, but instead on what they feel they're contributing to your firm's mission. And of course, even local candidates may decide to move on after five to ten years, simply because they want a fresh challenge.

Recruiting Remote Team Members

If you're considering hiring financial planners and other office staff to work remotely, then you need to ensure that your business has well-documented processes, superior management, a team with a strong work ethic, and the appropriate technological tools in place.

Process—Since your team members will not be able to walk down the hall to ask a question, your processes and procedures have to thoroughly detailed in writing. Firms that do not have well-documented processes are setting their remote employees—and all employees for that matter—up for failure. To enable success, new hires must know where to locate necessary information, and ideally they should have access to video and/or voice recordings explaining how to complete their daily tasks.

Management—Managers should try to spend as much face time with remote employees as possible, even if it's only for a few hours per year. Between these visits, have regularly scheduled virtual meetings. For example, my recruiting firm works as a virtual team and meets remotely on Mondays to discuss what we plan to accomplish in the week ahead. On Fridays, I hold short video or phone meetings with each team member to discuss where they surpassed their goals and where they may have fallen short. I also give them time to vent their frustrations and provide honest feedback on how they're feeling.

Team—Strive to build a team that will learn to trust each member without seeing them every day. As an owner, you must be able to trust your team, as well, because if you're constantly worried about what they're doing throughout the workday, it's not the right fit. That mental energy that you're expending could be better utilized elsewhere.

Tools—Assuming that you have the correct candidate and processes in place, the tools that you choose to employ will largely dictate whether a remote work environment will be successful for your firm. Here is a list of the tools that you should consider, many of which utilize a freemium pricing structure.

- **Slack**—Think AOL Instant Messenger on steroids. It can be integrated with Wunderlist (for task management) and a number of other applications. For many firms, Slack is a more efficient alternative to intraoffice emails.

- **Join.me**—This video conferencing and screen sharing software allows you to create custom URLs for your virtual team members. Suitable alternatives include Skype, Google Hangouts, and GoToMeeting.
- **iDoneThis**—This project accountability program sends an email indicating exactly what has been accomplished that day.
- **Evernote**—Designed for note taking, organizing, and archiving, Evernote will change the way that you organize your business. You can use it as an online storage unit for all of your projects, policies, and procedures, and it also allows your team members to collaborate in a single workspace and sync files across multiple devices.
- **LastPass**—This virtual password lockbox makes it easy to give access to all of your software systems to virtual employees, while not disclosing the actual passwords and login credentials. And if an employee were to leave your firm, you can instantly terminate access without having to change all of your firm-wide passwords.
- **ShareFile**—This is a robust, secure cloud-based file sharing program. Suitable alternatives include Box and Dropbox.

Firms that employ these strategies and utilize a remote workforce stand to have a significant competitive advantage in the fight for talent in the years to come. Furthermore, due to the more transient nature of today's workforce, these firms also have a greater chance of retaining top team members who may have to relocate due to a family illness, spousal job change, and so on.

CHAPTER 2

The Business Development Conundrum

When most financial planning firms are founded, the common development approach is to pursue every potential client possible. As the saying goes, "If they can fog a mirror, they're a prospect." This may be a sensible approach when starting out—after all you're just trying to keep the lights on—but as firms grow and develop recurring revenue streams, the pressure to constantly bring in new clients dissipates somewhat. Eventually, as firms become more established, the owners develop more strict criteria as to who they will accept as clients. Most commonly, this involves implementing minimums based on financial metrics such as assets to be managed, net worth, income, and referral potential.

Although this approach seems logical, it often leads to tension between firm owners and their team members who are required to develop new business. This is because the new business developers are required to grow their firms within minimums that even the firm owners themselves never faced! This is further complicated by the fact that many of the financial planning employees hired in the past never had "business development" listed as part of their job descriptions. Yet now, in an effort to sustain growth rates despite aging clientele and a depleting asset base, they're told that they will be evaluated based on business development as well as their other duties. In other words, employees who were hired to be technicians (minders and grinders), are now being required to source new clients (finders), and do so with minimums that even the owners never had to contend with when they started their businesses.

I've seen this cultural shift cause great upheaval within existing firms. If this dichotomy of high-minimum business development is left unaddressed for too long, resentment develops and eventually team members depart. This is especially true for next generation planners who feel they're being asked to do something that even the firm owners themselves did not have to do—bring in clients with lofty asset levels at the start of their careers. Unfortunately, not only are staff lost, but it's also more difficult to attract the best talent to replace those that have resigned when a firm takes this path.

Expecting New Hires to Develop Business

Although expecting new planners to generate some degree of business isn't necessarily unreasonable, problems will emerge if firm owners default to evaluating young new hires on the same standard that it took several decades for themselves to achieve. This misguided expectation and excess "sales" pressure, even within RIAs, is one of the leading reasons why young planners decide to leave the profession altogether. They end up viewing the financial planning industry as greedy and corrupt, focused only on gathering assets and chasing revenue without providing rewarding long-term prospects. Firms struggling with this should look to pivot by implementing the following strategies:

Recalibrate Expectations—Encourage new planners to network within their peer groups, which is a more level playing field, instead of trying to land a client twice to three times their age. Let them source a book of clients their own age, so they can grow old with them, as you have done with your clients over the years.

Revisit Minimums—If new planners approach you with a proposal or potential prospects that they want to bring aboard, seek common ground versus drawing a line in the sand.

Review Your Fee Structure—Objectively look at your fee structure and determine if it's conducive to developing your new planners and fostering their long-term growth. Rather than defaulting to upstream clients only, gauge what changes would be necessary to your fees in order to accommodate the emerging affluent clientele. If you don't have the infrastructure in place, consider utilizing a platform such as XY Planning Network.

Challenges of Hiring a Permanent Associate Planner

Another common challenge that I see firms struggle with is the dilemma of whether to hire a planner who will stay in the associate role permanently, or whether they should pursue a more traditional hire who will progress along a career path and eventually assume a lead planner role. The key considerations of hiring a permanent associate planner are as follows.

Opportunities of Hiring a Permanent Associate Planner

Ease of Management—Due to the finite nature of a permanent associate planner's career trajectory, the expectations should be less ambiguous since the scope of the role is limited and straightforward. As a firm owner, the "set it and forget it" management and training style is likely to work well in this setting. This frees up your time to focus on higher revenue generating activities like sourcing new clients.

Streamlined Screening Process—Since you don't have to try and foresee what the new hire will develop into with limited upfront knowledge, designing the candidate screening protocol should be clearer. For example, if the role of the associate planner is to create financial plans, then the screening and interviewing process should mainly entail the candidate proving to you that he or she can perform this activity.

Improved Hiring Cycle—Probably the most obvious benefit related to hiring a permanent associate planner is that if he or she stays in the position for a lengthy tenure, you do not have to find a replacement every few years and repeat the time-intensive hiring and training process that can drain your firm's valuable resources.

As a word of caution, even those who have promised you multiple times that they want to stay in the associate planner position indefinitely may still end up asking for a promotion in the future. Accordingly, if you pursue a permanent associate planner, you should specifically seek out candidates who have tried and/or failed in a lead planner role because that person will be less likely to ask for career advancement in the future.

Challenges of Hiring a Permanent Associate Planner

Not a Scalable Business Model—An associate planner serving in a behind-the-scenes role or permanent second chair is not capable of advising clients directly. This means that a permanent associate planner is not going to be a solution for lead planners or firm owners who are seeking to shift off "B-level" clients to reduce the number of relationships they manage.

Lack of Business Development—An ideal situation for most firm owners that I speak to is to groom an associate planner so that she can develop into a lead planner. This allows her to start working with existing clients independently and start bringing in clients of her own. This is much less likely to happen with permanent associate planners because they may have tried and failed at this part of the business in the past, or they may harbor certain fears related to these activities that they cannot overcome.

Reduced Talent Pool—Finding a qualified candidate that is seeking this somewhat unique role, in an already tight talent market, can be challenging and often frustrating for firm owners. There tends to be less movement of these types in the financial planning profession due to the fact that they are not seeking the next great opportunity and they're not interested in "seeing what else is out there." It's also worth noting that someone with limited career growth aspirations may lack the passion and motivation to do a great job in the role.

The candidates who are most successful serving as permanent associate planners are typically baby boomers and Gen X'rs who are not the primary breadwinners in their households. To a large degree, these long-term support positions have not been popular with Gen Y. As a firm owner, recognize that younger planners tend to be more ambitious and may not be content working for a firm that knowingly offers them no career advancement.

Challenges of Hiring an Entrepreneur

The consensus view from consultants and myself is that having a number of employees in an organization with overlapping skill sets doesn't make sense strategically. Despite this common sentiment, some firm owners inevitably decide to proceed down this path anyway. If that's the case, and you decide to hire a "mini-me"—in particular, one who has an entrepreneurial and rainmaker skill set similar to yours—be aware of the following:

- Candidates that have a rainmaker and entrepreneurial personality will not need you as much as others who don't have this skill set. After all, young rainmakers and entrepreneurs can always go start their own business— just as you probably did at their age! Therefore, getting these types of candidates to work for you can be challenging. If these candidates are true entrepreneurs like you, they probably have their own firms already or will be starting one in the near future.

- Entrepreneurial candidates are not going to be satisfied serving in support-type roles for long. If your goal is to simply hire someone to do a specific job indefinitely, there will be a mismatch. These types of candidates are looking for a *career*, not a job. If you're unable or unwilling to give them increased responsibilities, more client interaction, higher compensation, and career satisfaction, they will look for opportunities elsewhere within a few years.

- Don't be surprised if they push back on your ideas. Although this can contribute to your firm's growth if done in a professional, respectful way, this challenge of opinions can be a source of frustration for unsuspecting firm owners. If you say that you don't want to hire a "yes sir" or "yes ma'am" type of candidate, make sure that you mean it!

- Be prepared to provide these entrepreneurial candidates with an organizational chart, job description, expectations summary, compensation summary, and career path. They will want to know exactly what they need to do to advance through the career path as fast as possible. Don't lose good talent simply by being unprepared. But keep in mind, if you provide this information to those who you encourage to "think like an owner," after a while they will likely want to *become* an owner. If you're unwilling to provide an ownership stake, be careful what you ask for.

To avoid the aforementioned challenges, ask yourself the following five questions before considering an entrepreneurial hire.

1. What does your firm's career path look like for an entry-level hire? Are your expectations and time frames reasonable to allow an entrepreneurial candidate to advance through her career?

2. How will the new hire fit in with your existing company culture?
3. What work can the new hire do that you don't want to?
4. If you're hiring someone similar to yourself, what would your previous employer say it was like to manage you?
5. If you once left your employer to start your own firm, is your "mini-me" going to do the same?

CHAPTER 3

What New Planners Really Want

I was recently approached by a well-known financial planner who was experiencing frustration in trying to hire a qualified candidate to fill an open position. He asked me, "What do new planners really want in a position?" I thought this was an interesting question that needed to be addressed because often I find that one, or even both parties, cannot clearly articulate what they're seeking in an employment arrangement.

On the surface, new planners are seeking a position where they can learn and experience the business of financial planning firsthand because they can't acquire that education from a degree or certificate program. In an effort to provide more clarity, I've created the following summary based on hundreds of discussions that I've had over the last ten years with new financial planners. From my experience they are seeking the following:

- To work alongside an experienced financial planner in direct support of clients.
- To be fairly compensated and receive adequate training.

- To be given the opportunity to showcase the knowledge and skills they've learned through their education and internships.
- To be mentored so they can improve upon their existing knowledge base and eventually take on more responsibilities.
- To interact with clients through email, phone calls, and face-to-face meetings in order to refine their communication and soft skills.
- To use leading industry software to create financial plans for clients.
- To research investments and allocate client portfolios.
- To be exposed to all aspects of a financial planning business, including operations, IT, financial planning, and client services.
- To work in a warm and friendly environment where employees and their families come first.
- To obtain the CFP® designation and become involved in professional organizations.
- To be challenged by their employers, but treated fairly at all times.
- To be given the freedom and flexibility to voice their concerns, and for their ideas to be taken seriously.
- To be presented with growth opportunities and have a clear understanding of what is required to advance through their company's career path.

Are You Offering Growth Opportunities?

That last item on the list seems to carry the most weight with new planners, but what exactly constitutes a "growth opportunity" in a new financial planner's mind? To answer this question, I spoke with a number of CFP®

certificants, as well as those pursuing their CFP® certification. Each planner was still with the same firm where they started their career, each had between two to four years of professional experience, and each firm was an independent RIA with a minimum of $150 million in assets under management. The basic flow of our conversations went like this:

Candidate: *I mostly enjoy my firm and the people that I work with, but I'm also interested in seeing what other opportunities are available.*

CBrown: *Thanks for sharing that. Firms are hiring, but it's very difficult to find a good fit. From what I can tell from your resume, it appears that you have a pretty good job with a reputable company. Why do you want to know what else is out there?*

Candidate: *I'm looking for more growth opportunities than what are currently being offered here.*

CBrown: *What exactly do you mean by "growth opportunities"?*

Candidate: *[Various responses summarized] I want to keep improving upon my current skills plus develop new ones; I want to learn from others; I want to transition into more of a planning role; I want a more active role in client meetings; I want to bring in clients but my firm won't let me because they don't meet the firm minimum; I want to move up the organizational chart to garner more responsibility and compensation.*

CBrown: *There are firms out there offering this, but what is keeping you from doing this at your current firm?*

Candidate: *[Various responses summarized] I've had the same job responsibilities for a few years now and my firm will not let me advance in my career; The owner is too busy to provide any guidance or mentoring; My last name is not the same as the owner or the owner's kids who are in the business; Management is happy to have me remain in my current position indefinitely because I do quality work and meet their business needs; The owner will always see me as a "behind-the-scenes" person.*

CBrown: *This is common with independent financial planning firms, so don't think that by going to another firm you can avoid these altogether. Realize that I only know one side of the story, but I'm going to give the firm owner the benefit of the doubt and assume that if you're delivering, he or she would provide the items that you mentioned. Owners know how hard it is to find good employees, and if they've got one, they usually don't let them go very easily. Could it be that you aren't meeting expectations?*

Candidate: *Maybe, but nothing has come up in my reviews. Instead, promises are made with respect to the growth opportunities that I'm seeking, but there doesn't seem to be any action.*

At this point, it starts to become apparent that the lack of growth opportunities may lie with the firm rather than the candidate. The most important distinction that I see between the firms that effectively retain their planners and those who don't is how they view the money spent on staff. To paraphrase a popular Mark Tibergien observation, "Most firms view their payroll expense as a cost; the best firms look at that expenditure as an investment into an asset." In reality, for many firms, their human capital is the biggest asset they possess—if they account for it properly. The firms that understand this are always seeking new ways to ensure their planners are more than satisfied with their careers and growth opportunities. They are continuously investing in them for their mutual benefit, and in turn, this provides the necessary opportunities for these new planners to become "STARS." Here are a few simple ways these standout firms are achieving this:

- **Sophistication**—If a new planner is already meeting with clients, then providing the chance to work on increasingly complex client cases is an opportunity to improve her planning skills. If a new planner isn't currently meeting with clients, provide an occasion for her to do so. If you own a large firm, consider providing opportunities for employees to rotate internally to gain experience in multiple areas of your firm's operations. The cross-training is beneficial for your firm and its employees because it assists with organizational staffing needs as well as career path clarity. As a manager, it's important to know how to push your employees out of their comfort zones to drive them towards personal growth.

- **Training**—This step is crucial. Recently, one of my clients flew a new hire halfway across the country to spend a few weeks observing a comparable position with another firm. It spurred a number of new ideas and powerful discussion points within my client's firm. It also showed the new hire how committed the owner was to the training process and her professional growth.

- **Adaptability**—In the tightknit financial planning profession, word spreads quickly when planners feel like their firm truly wants to see them succeed in their careers and in life. These firms often attract more qualified candidates than they can possibly hire. To become one of these firms, simply asking your current employees what is important to them is a great first step. To demonstrate, I recently met a planner who wanted to pursue a PhD to focus on financial therapy and life planning because that was important to him. He thought it could add value to his firm, so he presented a proposal to the owner who decided to fully fund the degree and provide an accommodating work schedule. In turn, the planner feels more committed than ever to the firm because he recognized the investment they made in him.

- **Responsibility vs. Rewards**—From my conversations with new financial planners, they seem to prefer increased responsibility versus financial rewards. This has held true over the years, and I can personally attest to it. Early in my career, I was placed in a situation where I had to run a company for a few weeks. I wasn't fully qualified to do so, but my supervisor was unavailable, planning an important life event. Even though it was temporary, it was a substantial increase in responsibility. The opportunity motivated me to work even harder because I was entrusted to lead the company. It reaffirmed the fact that I was not going to be held to some arbitrary growth timeline. When my supervisor returned, he acknowledged that he "couldn't have done it without me," and this was worth more than any bonus that I ever received. I knew that I had made a difference and I was recognized for it.

- **Atmosphere and Culture**—A collegial and respectful atmosphere is one in which new planners are encouraged to share their ideas without fear of being discounted because of their short tenure with your firm. Firms that encourage thought leadership and actually mean it when they say that the status quo should be challenged are best positioned for long-term growth. In fact, new planners who feel their ideas are heard and are given an opportunity to explore those ideas, more often than not, describe those experiences as growth.

Consider focusing on these ideas if you haven't already, as a means of increasing the likelihood that your new planners will grow with you and not with a competing firm. If you think that you're offering this kind of environment already, confirm it by asking your employees what you can do differently to ensure they have the best growth opportunities possible.

CHAPTER 4

Crafting a Compelling Job Description

As a firm owner, there are several things that you can do to attract the best candidates, and having a compelling job description is at the top of the list. Often, the job description is the first interaction that a potential candidate will have with a firm, and making a good first impression is key. To help you draft a proper job description, or refine an existing one, we'll review the six main sections: Introduction, position overview, initial areas of responsibility, potential future areas of responsibility, qualifications, and benefits.

Section 1: Introduction

Keep the introduction focused on what's in it for the candidate. Describe how she can thrive and advance her career by joining your organization. Many of today's job descriptions are too heavily focused on the firm and its accomplishments. There's no need to use valuable space listing much of what can be found on your website and Form ADV. Instead, describe what type of candidate you're interested in, and what it takes to be successful at your firm.

What to avoid: Lengthy self-promoting diatribes that rarely make mention of the opportunity for the candidate. Trust me, they don't care all that much about how many awards you've won.

Section 2: Position Overview

This section serves as your mission statement for the new hire. Use it to paint a picture of what a typical day in the position would look like. Describe who on your team the candidate would be spending the most time with and what the job would entail on a daily basis. For some firms, this might be preparing financial plans, and for others it could be client service.

What to avoid: Going into too much detail.

Section 3: Initial Areas of Responsibility

This section explains what the new hire will be expected to do immediately upon joining your firm. Articulating these current responsibilities is vital because it lays the groundwork for setting role expectations, and it helps avoid any unwanted surprises. When explaining these responsibilities, it's fine to include the tasks that no one else at your firm wants to do, but it should be balanced with some greater responsibilities, as well. Remember that the top candidates are looking for interesting work that allows them to showcase their skills and work directly with clients. They know there won't be much opportunity for growth if they're scanning documents and researching cost basis for the majority of the day.

What to avoid: Listing every task that you could possibly want completed. If you've hired the right person, he or she will understand that in a small business environment, everyone has to pitch in at different times and engage in certain activities that weren't necessarily spelled out in the job description.

Section 4: Potential Future Areas of Responsibility

This section details what a new hire can expect if he or she meets or exceeds your expectations. It's a key section of the job description because it reinforces to the candidate that there are true growth opportunities available at your firm. It also serves to assuage the common fear that many candidates have, which is they will be stuck in the same role indefinitely. Although they will still have to deliver, it provides hope that there is something to work towards!

What to avoid: Listing roles and responsibilities that you have no intention of letting an employee actually perform.

Section 5: Qualifications

Your intention should be to set the framework for the skill set that you seek. To do this, list the skills that are necessary to succeed at the job. Keep in mind, the longer and more restrictive your list becomes, the smaller the pool of applicants will be. You may also scare away an applicant who may have been a great fit for your firm simply because he or she didn't meet one of the dozen items that you listed. From my experience, owners are better served by focusing on a candidate's passion for the profession, initiative, coachability, and positive attitude, rather than seeking out those who hold certain licenses and certifications.

What to avoid: An all-encompassing laundry list of wishes that describe your perfect candidate. Remember, perfect candidates probably don't exist, or if they do, they're probably already your competition!

Section 6: Benefits

This section needs to be thorough, but avoid replicating your employee handbook verbatim. New hires expect reasonable cash compensation, access to health insurance, and a retirement plan. Anything that you can offer above and beyond that is great and should be included because it sets you apart from your competitors.

What to avoid: Ignoring the benefits that other firms are offering to the same talent pool that you're both competing for.

Finally, be careful about overselling the position in an attempt to catch the eye of top talent. You risk developing a reputation for not delivering on the opportunities that you're offering. Financial planning is a small and growing profession, and word travels fast.

For a sample associate financial planner job description, see Appendix A.

Where to Seek Top Talent

Until the financial planning profession becomes more of a profession of choice for the younger crop of college graduates, finding qualified candidates will continue to be a challenge. As a financial planning recruiter, I'm often asked the question, "How do you find your candidates?" The short answer is that many of them find me or my company directly, due to our reputation and brand recognition within the industry. But if you own a typical financial planning firm that isn't continuously hiring, it can be difficult to rely on your brand and reputation alone to attract the best candidates for your job openings. With that in mind, here are four factors that you should consider when evaluating your online presence from the perspective of attracting future employees:

Website—Due to the lack of a popular and widely adopted job board for quality financial planning positions, many job seekers simply Google "Financial planning firms in [city name]." Thus, firms that have focused on search engine optimization (SEO) and are at the top of the Google search results in their respective cities are more likely to receive inquiries from prospective hires than their competitors. Of course, this assumes that you have a website that is up to par in the first place. If your website is lacking in design or function, it's going to be difficult to attract Gen X and Gen Y candidates to your firm. As a general rule, you should be willing to spend a few thousand dollars to overhaul your website, or at least update it, every few years.

Industry Media—The top candidates are reading the leading industry publications like *Investment News, Journal of Financial Planning, Financial Planning Magazine,* and *ThinkAdvisor.com*. They're looking for thought leaders and firm owners with interesting stories, whom they can contact for potential employment opportunities. Firms that are active in the various trade publications are able to cast a wider net and establish themselves as industry leaders, which is appealing to prospective hires. In other words, getting media exposure isn't just good for obtaining potential clients, but it also helps source prospective employees, too.

Social Media—Twitter, LinkedIn, and Facebook can be powerful tools for finding future employees. For example, when my company posts a new job opportunity, the combined 40,000+ Twitter followers between my company, New Planner Recruiting (@NewPlnrRec), and Michael Kitces (@MichaelKitces), along with the other social media platforms like Facebook, provide thousands of impressions to potential job candidates. And that doesn't account for the exponential increase in impressions if they "like" or "retweet" it.

Job Boards—The power of the internet makes it possible for firms to have their open positions viewed by thousands of prospective candidates, but it can be difficult trying to decide which job board, if any, to use. After all, a job board is only as good as the candidates that view it. To guide you, I've included the following chart that lists the most popular options available in the financial planning industry. The cost to post an open position ranges from free (with limited visibility) on Indeed, to several thousand dollars for prolonged listings on the CFP® Board Career Center. Visit the website provided for each job board to obtain current pricing information.

Job Board	Post Duration	Website
Career Builder	30 days	CareerBuilder.com
CFP® Board Career Center	30/60/90 days	CFP.net
Craigslist	30 days	Craigslist.com
eFinancialCareers	30 days	eFinancialCareers.com
Facebook	Varies	Facebook.com
Financial Planning Association	30 days	FPA.net
Glassdoor	30 days	Glassdoor.com
Indeed	Unlimited	Indeed.com
LinkedIn	30 days	LinkedIn.com
Monster	30 days	Monster.com
NAPFA	90 days	NAPFA.org
RIA NextGen	Varies	RIANextGen.com
Snagajob	30 days	Snagajob.com
Simply Hired	30 days	SimplyHired.com

To complement your online presence, you'll need a strong ground game, too. Here are several additional areas where you should focus your marketing efforts to attract the highest caliber financial planning talent:

Visit Schools—A representative from your firm should visit several schools in your area to help fill your talent pipeline. CFP® Board Registered Programs are saturated with prospective employers though, so the earlier you visit in the recruiting cycle, the better your chances of securing quality candidates will be.

Teach a Class—Volunteer to teach a CFP® class or give a guest lecture at a local university. This will grant you firsthand access to top performing students, rather than emailing professors and hoping they refer their best students to you (especially since some professors have their own firms and hire the top talent themselves). Realize, though, that just because a student performs well in the classroom, it doesn't necessarily mean that he or she will excel at your firm. Although teaching can be labor intensive, it's similar to other volunteer opportunities in the sense that you get out what you put in.

Become a Mentor—There are many ways to structure a mentorship. You can take the formal route and become part of a mentorship program that professional associations like the Financial Planning Association (FPA) and NAPFA offer, or you can simply find someone new to the profession and offer to serve as a mentor. Becoming a mentor means sharing the good, the bad, and the ugly about the profession and taking a genuine interest in the new planner's life.

Actively Participate—Becoming involved in your community—both locally and regionally—gives you substantially more opportunities to meet prospective candidates (and clients) for your firm. Furthermore, taking an active role in local chapters of professional associations, such as the FPA, can prove to be invaluable. When I started my career fresh out of college, I was the Career Development Director for the Dallas/Fort Worth chapter of the FPA. Because of this, many job seekers contacted me for employment opportunities, and in fact I was usually the first person they reached out to as they began their search. If a member of your firm serves in a similar volunteer position, that means the candidates would be coming to you!

Develop an Internship Program—Given the fierce competition for young talent, firms that have a structured internship program have a substantial competitive advantage. They're able to essentially "lock up" interns early on, who often go on to become full-time hires. If you're struggling to find suitable activities for interns to perform, consider having them document processes, compare various software packages, or develop content for a firm newsletter.

Utilize a Recruiting Firm—If the time it takes to invest in the previous strategies seems overwhelming, consider hiring a recruiting firm that can help find qualified candidates, and even run the hiring process altogether if necessary. Ideally, you'll work with a firm that has established relationships with a number of existing CFP® programs to maximize the potential for finding top talent. Costs will typically be between 20 to 35 percent of the first year's cash compensation, although some recruiting firms will charge a flat fee. In exchange for your payment, you'll save hours of time and avoid many of the negative consequences associated with a "bad hire," including excessive turnover.

Unfortunately, most financial planning firms have a more ad hoc recruiting strategy compared to the detailed plan that I've outlined. They simply wait until the last possible moment to begin the hiring process and are therefore subjected to a compressed timeline that leads to fewer, less qualified candidates. In order to ensure the continued success of your firm, I suggest combining the "boots on the ground" activities along with those that boost your online presence to proactively garner the attention of the qualified candidates needed to fill your recruiting pipeline.

CHAPTER 5

Letting Your Culture Recruit for You

Occasionally, when a new recruiting client comes on board, they will ask me how they should structure their compensation and benefits. Their questions usually revolve around salary, incentive bonuses, and perhaps health insurance and vacation time. When looking to attract talent, though, this focus on compensation and benefits can quickly become a Red Ocean of competitive fighting with other firms pursuing the same end goal. I suggest instead pursuing a Blue Ocean strategy of avoiding the competition altogether and creating something new—namely by focusing on your firm's *culture* as a key part of your overall compensation package.

To achieve this, start by focusing on the work-life balance of your employees. It's been well-documented that "strategic renewal," or daytime workouts, short afternoon naps, longer sleep hours, and more time away from the office boosts productivity, health, and morale. Tending to clients and taking care of their needs is hard work, and it's important for you and your staff to avoid burnout. These down times allow the mind to gain a different perspective, stoke creativity to solve difficult problems, and boost energy levels. Consider allowing short breaks throughout the day so your staff can go for walks, have lunch away from their workstations, and even take power naps—yes, some companies allow this! If your employees complete their assigned work for the day, let them knock off a few hours early. If they performed well on a project, acknowledge it, provide an overview of their next project, and give them extra time outside the office to think about how best to approach it.

Here are eight additional ideas that I've seen firms employ, and have even experienced in my own career, which have assisted in building an employee-centric culture:

1. Place a pool table, air hockey table, or video game console in your break room. Sometimes employees need to blow off steam and just have a few moments of fun prior to getting back to the grind. Also consider inexpensive ideas like hallway putting contests, '80s tie day, and streaming NCAA tourney games in March.

2. Buy lunch for your employees and allow them time away from their desks to share a meal and bond with their coworkers. This promotes synergy and reinforces to employees that it's not always about the bottom line. Better yet, if you just signed on a large new client or had a successful meeting, close the office early and take everyone out for happy hour. Your employees will remember these types of things and will pass them along to their network, who could potentially be future employees. (A long time ago, I had an employer promise during my interview that we would stop work early sometime and go play basketball. I can't remember what my

salary was at that job, but I do remember that we never did play basketball. For this reason, and quite a few others, I didn't feel comfortable referring my network when the firm was hiring.)

3. Allow your employees to work from home for the day if they don't have any in-office meetings. Telecommuting and open vacations are being utilized successfully by many firms today. Keep in mind, with advances in technology, it doesn't necessarily matter *where* your employees are working, as long as they're available to clients and the work is getting done.

4. Provide annual passes to a local entertainment venue, memberships to a gym, and tickets to local sporting events. Find out what's important to your employees before doing this.

5. Allow employees to dedicate two hours each week to work on whatever interests them. The following week, have them discuss their work and how it can benefit your firm. You will be empowering and challenging your employees to be creative and increase their skill set. If you're concerned that your employees will venture too far off topic, consider providing broad categories from which they can choose, such as marketing, technology, and client processes.

6. Create internal contests with small prizes. There's nothing wrong with creating some friendly competition and showing your team that it's not all about work all of the time.

7. Host regularly scheduled get-togethers for employees and their families. The spouses and close family members of your employees are your biggest allies when long work hours can make them begin to question if they've found a good culture fit.

8. Offer a sabbatical program so employees can take extended periods of time off as needed. This is being offered by a growing number of firms who have had employees resign in the past, leaving them scrambling to shore up their organizational chart.

From my experience, every firm says they have a great culture, but few truly do. To recruit the top candidates, you need a compelling story and an employee-friendly culture so that your team members could never imagine working anywhere else.

Ensure Your Firm is Tech Savvy

Over the last few years, I've noticed an increased tendency for candidates to focus on what technologies firms are using before making their final commitment. I've even witnessed firms lose qualified candidates because they lacked the proper technology infrastructure. With that in mind, I'd like to challenge you to review your current technologies to see if your firm is meeting the mark. How would you rate yourself in the following categories?

Software Utilization—Believe it or not, I still come across firms that do not use any type of financial planning software or customer relationship management (CRM) software. The prior is somewhat understandable, especially if there is not a focus on comprehensive financial planning, but relying on Outlook, Excel, or nothing at all for CRM is concerning to say the least. Apart from potentially being non-compliant, it virtually eliminates a firm's chance of attracting the best and brightest candidates. New planners are being trained on the most popular CRM programs like Redtail, Junxure, Tamarac, and Salesforce, along with the top financial planning programs like Moneytree, MoneyGuidePro, eMoney, and NaviPlan. So naturally they tend not to be as excited when they learn that a firm uses custom Excel spreadsheets or no software at all. If you're considering migrating to one of the aforementioned programs, hiring a new planner and letting her take the lead on research, selection, and implementation will help with both employee retention and firm innovation.

Website Appearance—Gone are the days of viewing your website as simply "an online brochure." Ideally, you should be updating your website every three to five years to give it a fresh new look. To supplement your traditional website, consider having a professional LinkedIn profile, Twitter handle, and Facebook page that includes your picture, because prospective candidates and clients will review these to decide whether they can envision themselves working with you.

Hardware Tools—Consider upgrading your office computers every few years, since microchip performance tends to improve sharply every 18 to 24 months. Also, be sure to provide large monitors for your team members, and possibly multiple screens as well, to increase productivity. As I travel on the conference circuit, I've noticed a trend shifting away from bulky laptops and iPads to hybrids such as Microsoft's Surface Pro and Lenovo's Yoga Pro. Devices such as these are worth considering as you visualize how work gets done in your firm today, and how it will get done in the future as hardware adaptability and working remotely become more important to next generation planners.

Industry experts recommend that annual spending on technology should be a minimum of 3 to 10 percent of a firm's revenue. In the end, utilizing emerging technologies will make your organization more efficient and ensure that you'll be at the forefront of the industry. As you consider increasing your technology budget, remember that current and future team members want to be part of a technology-centric culture and not stuck at what they perceive to be an "old school firm" that is unwilling to change.

CHAPTER 6

Hiring for Effort

When contemplating staffing decisions for your firm, elements such as timing, interest, philosophy, expectations, compensation, personality, and skill set all have to align for you to make a good hire. So how do you know which items to focus on to ensure that you're making the best possible hire? Unfortunately, there's no foolproof proverb in employee selection, but I've found that hiring based on the demonstrated efforts of a candidate is a leading indicator of success—and this includes the effort they put into the job search process itself!

In a typical year, my team will review over five thousand resumes, and many are not worth a second look. Furthermore, there are ones that tend to be filled with ambiguities, overstatements, and stretches. For these reasons, making a hiring decision based on the resume and interview alone can be problematic. Instead, you need to also focus on intangibles like the effort exerted by candidates during the hiring process.

Here are a few leading examples of candidates that we recommended to firm owners and were subsequently hired based on effort:

- A candidate submitted her response to our mock financial planning exercise at 3 A.M. on a Tuesday morning. It's not all that rare to receive candidate submissions in the middle of the night, however we later found out that she had the final exam for her retirement planning class scheduled for 1 P.M. on Monday, and the final exam for her insurance class scheduled for Tuesday at 11 A.M. When I asked why she took the approach that she did, she simply responded that she was interested in the opportunities we had presented and did not want to delay the process. Rest assured, I do implore candidates to focus on their courses and only work on the requirements for our hiring process when they have time, but this was an exceptional candidate as the effort showed.

- Another candidate submitted a very thorough and accurate financial pan, which is a required step in our candidate evaluation process. While this alone is fairly common, the candidate not only completed the plan using our required software, but he also downloaded a separate software suite, completed the same plan again, and provided an analysis of the variances from the outputs of the two programs. When I asked the candidate why he did so much more than was required, he replied that he wanted to ensure that the client received accurate advice, and he wanted to build his skills to become more versatile.

- Finally, a candidate who was working part-time while taking a full load of college classes completed our entire screening process in two days. To thoroughly vet candidates for firm owners, our process includes multiple interviews, a work-style profile, financial planning exercises, and more, which candidates must complete on their own time. On average, it takes candidates about two weeks to complete it all. Yet, in this case, the candidate not only completed the process in two days, but plowed through without even asking what the typical timeframe was, as many candidates do. When I asked the candidate what motivated her to complete the work so quickly, she said that the exercises were challenging and she wanted to get a head start on the competition.

Unfortunately, the efforts displayed by these three candidates is not typical, and sadly, with today's talent squeeze, a good number of candidates are hired in our profession without exerting much effort at all. It's only later that firms realize that when candidates don't exert more than the minimum during the hiring process, they're unlikely to go above and beyond in their actual jobs. Why is this so critical? Because it's estimated that the financial cost of a bad hire is between one to three times the departing employee's salary, which does not even take into account intangible effects such as detrimental impacts to culture, morale, and employee confidence.

Indicators of a Candidate's Future Success

There are a number of traits and characteristics that candidates possess which serve as indicators of their future success as financial planners. In addition to technical ability, look for these "SPECIAL" markers of success:

- <u>S</u>ense of Urgency—While most candidates think they have this, few actually do. Unfortunately, having a burning desire to complete assignments as soon as possible so that others are not kept waiting is a rarity. When assessing candidates for your firm, be sure to monitor how long it takes them to reply to your requests for information, and whether they display a sense of urgency during the hiring process. This will tell you a great deal about how they might react to urgent client requests if they were hired by your firm.

- **Passion for the Profession**—Simply asking candidates why they chose financial planning as a career can give ample insight into their passion for the profession. But realize that those who give the standard response that they want to "help people" could have become doctors, lawyers (well, maybe), accountants, etc., so it's imperative to drill down in an effort to find their true motivation. Candidates that discuss their desire to alter someone's life for the better or describe how they plan to impact the financial planning profession are the ones you're looking for.

- **Empathy**—It can be challenging for a client-facing financial planner to succeed if he or she has difficulty understanding and relating to the feelings of others. After all, money can be a very emotional topic for clients, and candidates will struggle in their careers unless they can develop some level of empathy. To evaluate this, have candidates write a response to a mock client who asks for advice pertaining to a traumatic situation she's experiencing.

- **Communication Skills**—Developing rapport, earning trust, and providing advice is the heart of financial planning. When interviewing candidates, you'll quickly get a feel for whether their speaking and writing styles, presence, and advice delivery style can be effective with your clients. If at first glance you don't feel confident about their communication skills, consider what they could become with the proper coaching. You can also explore tools and training programs like Money Quotient, Kinder Institute of Life Planning, and Sudden Money Institute, which are designed to assist financial planners in creating deeper bonds with clients and becoming more effective communicators.

- **Introspection**—Socrates said, "Know thyself," but alas few people do. Sometimes asking candidates about their daily routines can shed some light on this, however. You can also assess their self-awareness through personality assessments such as StrengthsFinder and DISC. Candidates that ask for feedback, set goals, create bucket lists, spend time meditating, etc., tend to have a more introspective nature.

- **Attitude**—Generally, you want to hire candidates with positive attitudes who will work well with others. They should be motivated by learning from you and helping build your business (which they could end up acquiring at some point in the future). I encourage you to include in your job postings the expectation that candidates have a "no job is beneath me" attitude, which will cut down on the time wasted on entitled candidates. You should also ask about any type of team sports experience the candidates may have, because that is often synonymous with being able to work well with others, receive constructive criticism, and demonstrate effort that is above and beyond the minimum.

- **Listening**—Even though a lack of listening skills is mostly associated with new planners, there are experienced planners who struggle with this, as well. I can attest to this because when I attend conferences and meet planners for the first time, it amazes me how many of them immediately begin talking about themselves. At the end of our conversations I know everything about them, but they know very little about me.

   Fake listening is a problem, too, which I characterize as asking a question to be polite, but not being engaged in the response. During candidate interviews, I will often share a story or random fact and then ask questions about it a few minutes later to gauge how well the candidate was listening. A well-respected planner once told me that she strives to become almost trance-like when a client is speaking, to be sure that she is connecting with every word being spoken. That is the attitude that all planners should have.

CHAPTER 7

The Art and Science of Screening Candidates

As a firm owner, hiring a financial planner who is the right fit is both an art and a science. When dealing with entry-level candidates with no prior work history, it can be difficult to determine who will be a great hire and produce a positive return on investment. Further complicating matters is the fact that there are drastic differences in basic skill level between the graduates of various financial planning programs across the country. For these reasons, I recommend implementing the following 7-stage candidate screening process to help assess the core areas of each candidate's capabilities.

Stage 1: Resume Review

It should come as no surprise that the first step to screening candidates is reviewing their resumes. If you're using job boards to cultivate interest, set up an auto-response with instructions for submitting in order to deter the serial job applicants who are nothing more than time wasters. You should consider having candidates record videos of themselves explaining why they want the job you're offering to accompany their resumes. This will make it easier for you to determine if there is a potential culture, philosophy, work style and career fit for each candidate.

- Tip: Monitor who follows submission guidelines, who does the minimum work required, and who goes beyond the minimum. Focus your attention on the internships, extracurricular and leadership activities, and volunteerism sections of each resume, and don't forget to watch for spelling and grammatical errors, too.

- Time frame: You should review resumes and contact candidates within one week to schedule an interview or inform them that you're declining to do so. *For a sample candidate rejection letter, see Appendix B.*

Stage 2: Initial Interview

Typically held via phone or video chat (Google Hangout, Skype, etc.), the initial interview is meant for you to get a sense of the candidate's communication style, how she responds to your questions, and what questions she asks. Consider asking some of the same life planning questions that you ask clients to get a sense of her commitment and passion for financial planning. Also make sure that the candidate has a general familiarity with the following six points.

1. How financial planning firms serve clients, including the basic steps of the financial planning process.
2. How financial planning firms earn revenue.

3. The differences between commission-based and fee-only financial planning.

4. Professional terms, legislation, and acronyms such as ADV, fiduciary, broker/dealer, FINRA, SEC, and Dodd-Frank.

5. Basic economic concepts and their global and domestic implications.

6. The differences between active and passive investment management.

- Tip: When arranging the initial interview, have the candidate call you at a specific time to gauge how organized and timely she is. Don't leave it open ended, such as, "Call me any time in the afternoon."

- Time frame: Ideally, the initial interview should be scheduled no longer than a week from your reply to the candidate's resume inquiry (two weeks from first contact).

Stage 3: Computer Skills Test

The majority of resumes that I review specify that the candidate is "proficient" and/or an "expert" in something—usually the Microsoft Office Suite programs. Unfortunately, even amongst these candidates, skill sets vary significantly. Therefore, it's necessary to delve further into each candidate's level of proficiency by having them complete a basic computer skills test. This assessment should include a few of the fundamental computer tasks that the candidate would be expected to perform immediately upon being hired.

- Tip: If candidates claim to be "proficient" or "expert" at something, make them prove it!

- Time frame: The computer skills test should be administered within a week of the initial interview (three weeks from first contact).

Stage 4: Personality and Conative Assessment

Depending on the size of your firm and how intensive your recruiting process is, consider adding a personality and conative assessment component to help get a glimpse of the candidate's motivational and behavioral aspects. Use tools such as Profile XT, DISC, StrengthsFinder, or Kolbe, but be careful viewing this as a panacea. Personality profiles are best viewed as a small part of a larger, more comprehensive screening process. (Personality assessments are discussed in detail in the next chapter.)

- Tip: If you're going to perform a personality assessment, be sure to do it before moving on to Stage 5. Otherwise, you risk making up your mind based on the rest of your interactions with the candidate and essentially ignoring the findings of the assessment.

- Time frame: The personality assessment should be administered concurrently with the computer skills test (three weeks from first contact).

Stage 5: Cognitive Exercises

Just because a candidate may have graduated from a financial planning program doesn't guarantee that he or she can answer planning-related questions at the level you're expecting. To test this, compile a list of client questions that you've recently received and ask the candidate to answer them, or draw questions from the list provided below. Ideally, your questions should include all of the qualitative and quantitative areas of financial planning that you advise clients on. Have the candidate write a thorough response to each question to help you gain a better understanding of the thought process and rationale behind each answer.

1. Should a client contribute to a Roth or Traditional IRA?
2. When should a client consider a Roth conversion?
3. What vehicle should a client use to fund her child's college education?
4. Should a client withdraw investment funds to pay off her mortgage early?
5. Should a client select the lump sum or annual payment option from her pension?
6. What benefits should a client select during her employer's open enrollment period?
7. What type of life insurance should a client purchase, and for what amount?
8. Should a client lease or purchase a car? Rent or buy a home?

- Tip: Time the exercise to see how the candidate responds under pressure.

- Time frame: The cognitive exercises should be administered concurrently with the computer skills test and the personality assessment (three weeks from first contact).

Stage 6: Financial Plan Construction

It's crucial that a candidate understands how to gather and input data, double check her work, create specified reports, and analyze data to answer client questions. Have the candidate create a financial plan using the software that you employ, and monitor whether she plunges in or reads the instructions and watches tutorials first. This will provide valuable insight into her learning style.

- Tip: Have the candidate complete a case that closely resembles your ideal client profile.

- Time frame: The financial plan construction should be administered concurrently with the computer skills test, personality assessment, and cognitive exercises (three weeks from first contact).

Stage 7: Final Interview

If the candidate has made it through to this stage, spend time discussing any weaknesses that may have been uncovered through the hiring process. (If the candidate is remote, be sure to arrange an on-site interview, and be prepared to cover travel-related expenses such as airfare, a rental car, meals, and hotel accommodations. You should never hire a candidate without first meeting in-person!) Bring up any gut concerns that you have and be prepared to discuss an employment offer if all goes well. Also consider having multiple team members meet with the candidate to give her more exposure to other personalities at your firm, and to give you additional sources of input before making your final decision.

- Tip: Pay close attention to see if the candidate responds well to you, but interacts poorly with your staff.

- Time frame: The final interview should be scheduled within one week of the financial plan construction (four weeks from first contact). Realize that candidates swing mentally and emotionally from feeling extremely excited about an opportunity, to feeling as if you're not interested—so do not prolong the process. The probability of having a candidate accept your offer and not go elsewhere decreases over time.

For a sample final interview agenda, see Appendix C.

Avoiding the "Stud to Dud" Hire

Many firm owners that I talk to admit to being guilty of hiring the "stud to dud" candidate at some point in their careers. The candidate shined during the interview process, but failed to deliver as expected. In fact, this is one of the leading reasons why firm owners hire professional recruiters. Although there's no foolproof way to completely eliminate this occurrence, there are some common behavioral biases that can unwittingly impact the interview process. Here I will identify those biases and explain how to avoid them.

Consistency Bias—The consistency bias is the general inclination that all interviews needs to be uniform. While you should take a structured approach to interviews and ask (mostly) the same questions to each candidate, realize that you may have to go off script occasionally. For example, a candidate once told me that she used to work in a university call center trying to secure alumni donations, so I put her on the spot and asked her to pitch me on why I should donate. Not all candidates had her work history, and if I had not explored further I would have missed an opportunity to gain additional insight into her skill set.

Familiarity Bias—The familiarity bias suggests that if you're more familiar with one candidate over another, you may have a natural bias towards them because of the comfort of familiarity. This is an easy trap to fall into due to our empathetic nature as financial planners. To avoid this, you should strive to ensure that all candidates endure the same level of scrutiny during the interview process, and be sure to deal in facts as much as possible. For example, you may take notes such as, "The candidate was on time for her appointment, answered questions thoroughly, researched the firm, and asked probing questions about the job." Also consider having another team member conduct the interview if you know that you're prone to this bias.

Anchoring Bias—The anchoring bias is the general tendency to rely too heavily on the first piece of information received (the "anchor") when making decisions. For example, if you're interviewing a candidate and notice that she has listed an impressive accomplishment on her resume, you may be inclined to use that limited piece of appealing information as an excuse not to ask difficult questions to see if she'll be a good fit for your firm. (Think of the summa cum laude graduate from a prestigious Ivy League school who has no idea what a dividend is!) To avoid this bias, have each candidate complete the cognitive exercises outlined in Stage 5 of the previous section.

CHAPTER 8

Personality Assessments 101

Contrary to popular belief, qualities that are most easily measured, such as GPA, GMAT/GRE score, and performance on the CFP® Certification Exam, aren't necessarily the best indicators of a candidate's future success with your firm. Instead, the best predictors of a candidate's success are her motivation, coachability, attitude, communication, and work style. All of these can typically be described and understood through a quality personality assessment.

Although you can gain a fair amount of insight into one's personality through interviews, personal encounters, and observances in various settings, a personality profile is a worthwhile tool because it helps you get a better sense of how a person is wired. In some cases, it will reinforce what your gut is already telling you, but in other instances, the rigor, structure, and consistency of a formal personality assessment can reveal opportunities or concerns that may have otherwise been missed. Due to the seemingly endless number of assessments available, finding the right one can be daunting. Provided is an overview of the most common assessments that I administer, and the potential benefits and drawbacks of each.

Assessment	Questions	Cost	Length
DISC	24 forced choice	~$40	20 minutes
StrengthsFinder	177 forced choice	Varies	40 minutes
Caliper	150 forced choice and various others	~$195	90 minutes
Profile XT	247 forced choice and various others	~$250	60 minutes

- **DISC (Dominance, Influencing, Steadiness, Compliance)**—This tool provides a useful explanation and comparison of the respondent's adapted versus natural behavioral styles. When reviewing a candidate's DISC profile, observe how closely the natural and adapted styles match each other. The wider the discrepancy, the more adapting a person has to do which leads to increased strain in the work environment. The evaluation report provides keys to managing and motivating the respondents and guidelines for an ideal work environment. These can assist with onboarding, integrating, and coaching. The Success Insights Wheel classifies respondents based on their DISC scores, which can help you assess the strengths and weaknesses of your overall team. Available at TTISuccessInsights.com.

- **StrengthsFinder**—This tool is timed to keep respondents from overthinking the questions in an effort to secure a purer result. The evaluation report contains much of the same information as DISC, but focuses on each respondent's top five personality themes, such as Achiever, Learner, Maximizer, etc. It provides a narrative similar to DISC, but gives the respondents questions to ponder after each theme for self-reflection and professional development. As an interviewer, you can use these questions to delve deeper into certain areas as needed. Available at StrengthsFinder.com.

- **Caliper**—This assessment is similar to DISC, but also has a cognitive component, as well. Cost wise, it's one of the most expensive due to its thoroughness and sheer length (90 minutes), which is a great deterrent for the less serious candidates. The abstract reasoning, ego strength, urgency, and accommodation sections are among the most helpful attributes to study. These provide insight into a respondent's cognitive ability, capability to take constructive criticism without getting defensive, ability to complete tasks quickly, and capacity to work well with others. Caliper also includes a job matching function, which allows the interviewer to establish performance metrics which scores each respondent on position fit. Available at CaliperCorp.com.

- **Profile XT**—Similar to Caliper, this tool includes a cognitive measure and overall job matching feature. However, the evaluation report is longer than Caliper's and includes more detail. There are six sections to this assessment and due to its length (247 questions), it can serve as a deterrent for candidates who aren't fully committed. Pay close attention to the attitude, manageability, and decisiveness categories for insight on the likelihood that a respondent will have a positive attitude, follow established policies, and efficiently make decisions. Available at ProfilesInternational.com.

The benefit of these assessments is they measure many different aspects of a candidate's personality, but deciphering the results can be difficult. Due to their complexity, they are best administered and explained by a trained expert. If you decide to include one of these tools in your recruiting process, I urge you to administer the test early in the process before you've formed any biases toward the candidate. Otherwise you'll find yourself rationalizing, justifying, or completely ignoring the results.

Understanding the Kolbe Assessment

Now that we've reviewed several common personality assessments that measure the affective (feeling) and cognitive (thinking) parts of the mind, we'll now focus on a tool that measures the conative (doing) part of the mind—the Kolbe assessment.

With Kolbe, the focus is on understanding respondents' intrinsic knack for how they get things done, which is certainly consequential to a successful hire. The Kolbe assessment includes 36 forced choice questions that take approximately 20 minutes to complete. A 13-page evaluation report is generated after the assessment, which details the four action modes: Fact Finder, Follow Thru, Quickstart, and Implementor. These modes are driven by instincts, and represent the primary ways that respondents think through and solve problems. Each mode is measured on a scale from 1 to 10, and respondents are labeled as Preventative (1–3), Accommodating (4–6), and Initiating (7–10). As the labels suggest, the continuum spans from preventing problems to initiating solutions.

Further detail on the four Kolbe action modes is provided as follows:

Fact Finder (FF)—This mode provides insight into how comfortable a respondent is with details. Needless to say, being detail oriented is a critical trait for new planners who are expected to gather and analyze client data. I've witnessed a great deal of conative stress in this mode between firm owners who might be Preventative FFs and their new planners who might be Initiating FFs. The new planner wants to share all of the details for a particular task while the owner/supervisor would prefer to know the bottom line only. As a firm owner, make sure that your staff knows how you prefer to receive information. And the next time one of your employees repeatedly asks questions about a task that you've assigned, remember that it might not be a "Gen Y thing" but rather how he or she is instinctively wired.

Follow Thru (FT)—Not to be confused with "follow through," this mode shows how a respondent arranges and designs, and how much structure she prefers. Even in the most customizable situations, financial planning is heavily process driven, at least if you're doing it successfully and profitably. Because of this, firms benefit from process-oriented employees. Plus, having an Initiating FT on your team is valuable if you find yourself coming up with many big ideas but need help implementing them.

Quickstart (QS)—This mode examines how likely a person is to take uncalculated risks. Typically, financial planning firm owners are entrepreneurs who tend to be Initiating QS and are at their best when they're innovating, experimenting, and improvising. These are terrific attributes for an owner whose job it is to keep the firm running and growing, but support staff and financial planners may be at the other end of the continuum, causing frustration for many firm owners. I tend to hear something to the effect of, "My employees are resisting change, moving too slowly, and not taking initiative!" From planners, I often hear, "The owner is changing things all the time, giving me unrealistic deadlines, and I can't predict what he will do next!" A healthy balance should be struck because an Initiating QS firm owner needs a respectful level of push back from Preventative QS employees because not all innovations and ideas are good ones. Similarly, Preventative QS employees need an Initiating QS firm owner to keep them from getting too complacent.

Implementor (IM)—This mode is not to be misconstrued as a person who "can get the job done and get it implemented." Instead, it revolves around the instinct to construct a handcrafted, solid solution. Think of an Initiating IM as someone who is comfortable creating concrete solutions and prototypes, while a Preventative IM is more abstract and prefers to visualize rather than construct. Most financial planners are in the Preventative and Accommodating areas of Implementor unless they happen to come from an industrial background. If a new hire will be responsible for your firm's computer hardware, or will be required to integrate various programs in your back office, look for an Accommodating or Initiating IM.

Realize that Kolbe measures how a respondent *prefers* to take action, and it's not meant to suggest that adaption cannot occur. On the contrary, most everyone has the ability to adapt, but the key is to identify one's conative energy and then use it in the most purposeful way. I administer the Kolbe assessment to all of my candidates and clients, as well as those who want me to serve as their financial planner. For the minor time commitment and nominal financial cost, I'm able to better understand who I'm working with so I can communicate as efficiently and effectively as possible. Used properly, Kolbe can help you place new hires where their innate talents will flourish.

CHAPTER 9

Compensating New Planners

Properly structuring the compensation levels for your firm is vital to sustaining long-term growth. Set compensation levels too low and you can end up with an office full of average performers. On the other hand, if you set compensation levels too high, you might find yourself with a team motivated solely by money, who do not believe in the mission or vision that you've set forth. While there's no one-size-fits-all solution, my work with over two hundred financial planning firms has allowed me to observe certain trends that set firms up for continued success, as well as others that lead to disgruntled employees and high staff turnover.

The most common question that I'm asked when speaking at conferences is, "How much should I pay my new planner?" I liken this question to a prospective client walking into your office and asking, "How much money will I need to retire?" There are many factors at play, such as your firm's geographic location, staff size, revenue, assets under management, experience, designations/licenses, and education. But I promise to do better than the typical financial planner blanket answer of "it depends," and give you tangible guidelines to consider.

Let's first review the three main components of overall compensation, which are base compensation, incentive compensation, and employee benefits.

- **Base Compensation**—Defined as remuneration paid to an employee to complete the tasks required for a job, this is individual-based compensation. I've seen new planners being paid as little as $24,000 per year, all the way up to $75,000 per year. However, the majority are in the $40,000 to $55,000 range. This assumes an entry-level associate planner position that is usually salaried, with little to no business development requirements. Naturally, as an associate planner gains experience and becomes certified, her pay increases. Across the board, here is the annual base compensation that I commonly observe for an entire office staff.

  1. Administrative assistant: $30,000 to $50,000
  2. Office manager: $45,000 to $80,000
  3. Operations manager: $65,000 to $130,000
  4. Client services associate: $30,000 to $60,000
  5. Associate financial planner: $40,000 to $55,000
  6. Lead financial planner: $90,000 to $125,000
  7. Partner: $150,000 to $200,000+

- **Incentive Compensation**—This type of compensation allows employees to financially participate in the overall success of the firm. Incentive compensation can be structured a number of different ways and based on several different measures, such as firm revenue, number of financial plans written, client satisfaction survey results, new business development, and so on. Whatever measure you decide to use, make sure that the metrics to achieve it are clearly defined and attainable. Use incentive compensation to motivate your employees to get the results that you want. In most cases, I think an incentive target of 10 percent of base compensation is reasonable, and I am a proponent of tying this compensation to firm revenue. (Paying out 1 percent of firm revenue is typical for small to mid-size firms.)

- **Employee Benefits**—Sometimes referred to as "non-financial compensation," employee benefits are intended to enhance the other two areas of compensation already mentioned. On average, employee benefits make up 9 to 12 percent of total employee compensation and cost employers $4,500 per year for each employee. Employee benefits such as health insurance, retirement plans with a company match, and paid vacations are standard. Other benefits that you might want to consider providing include a travel budget, clothing allowance, cell phone plan, membership dues to professional associations, continuing education reimbursement, tuition reimbursement, a conference and training budget, staff retreats, sporting event tickets, personal financial planning, parking allowance, and group disability, dental, and life insurance. Other benefits that may be particularly popular with the Gen Y cohort include gym memberships, concert tickets, flextime, dual computer monitors, cell phones and tablets, and a solid supply of energy drinks and healthy snack foods.

In addition to these three main components of compensation, if you're planning to relocate your new hire then you should be prepared to offer additional benefits such as a moving allowance (I've seen up to $5,000), temporary housing, a signing bonus to offset breaking rental or lease contracts, a travel allowance to be used to visit family back home, and a housing stipend to offset increased housing costs if your firm is located in an expensive area. (I realize this list may be causing some of you to roll your eyes, but this is the reality of where our profession stands today in the fight for talent!)

For a sample compensation summary and offer letter, see Appendices D and E, respectively.

Compensation Packages That Led to Accepted Offers

Provided below are examples of firms that made competitive offers that were accepted by candidates. Keep in mind, this is cash compensation data only, and assumes a retirement plan with a 3 percent match, and health insurance coverage where the employer pays 50 percent of the premiums.

East Coast
- North Carolina: A firm with $200 to $500 million AUM offered a CFP® with 3-years' experience $58,000 per year plus up to 12 percent of base pay in incentive compensation.
- Washington, D.C.: A firm with $1 to $2 billion AUM offered a CFP® with 3-years' experience $60,000 per year plus a bonus based on a proprietary formula, estimated to be up to 33 percent of base pay after one year.
- Northern New Jersey: A firm with $100 to $400 million AUM offered a candidate who recently passed the CFP® exam, and had one year of experience, $64,000 per year plus a $5,000 bonus.

- Miami, FL: A firm with $500 million to $1 billion AUM offered a CFP® with 3-years' experience $63,000 per year plus up to 10 percent in incentive bonuses.

West Coast
- San Francisco, CA: A firm with $1 to $2 billion AUM offered a CFP® with 3-years' experience $75,000 per year plus a bonus of up to 10 percent of base pay.
- Northern California: A firm with $100 to $400 million AUM offered a candidate with 2-years' experience $73,000 per year plus a $10,000 bonus.

Fly Over States
- Houston, TX: A firm with $100 to $400 million AUM offered a CPA with 4-years' audit experience and no financial planning experience $75,000 per year plus a $5,000 bonus upon passing the CFP® exam.
- Houston, TX: A firm with $100 to $250 million AUM offered a career changer who completed the CFP® coursework $58,000 per year plus up to 15 percent in incentive bonuses.
- Atlanta, GA: A firm with $100 to $400 million AUM offered a new college graduate $40,000 per year plus a $3,000 signing bonus and a $2,500 bonus for passing the CFP® exam. In addition, the firm offered a 10 percent annual increase in base compensation for each of the first two years.
- Ohio: A firm with $200 to $500 million AUM offered a new college graduate $42,000 per year, with an increase to $45,000 upon passing the CFP® exam, and an additional increase to $53,000 upon being eligible to use the CFP® mark.

Compensation Packages That Led to Rejected Offers

The following offers were declined by candidates because they were deemed too low or non-competitive in the local market.

- Indiana: A firm with $100 to $400 million AUM offered a CFP® with 3-years' experience $53,000 per year.
- Phoenix, AZ: A firm with $200 to $500 million AUM offered a new college graduate $39,000 per year.
- San Francisco, CA: A firm with $500 million to $1 billion AUM offered a CFP® with 3-years' experience $60,000 per year.
- Houston, TX: A firm with $100 to $250 million AUM offered a career changer who completed the CFP® coursework $55,000 per year plus up to 15 percent in incentive bonuses. In addition, the firm offered a $2,000 education bonus and a $2,000 per year salary increase upon passing the CFP® exam.
- Alabama: A firm with $100 to $400 million AUM offered a new college graduate $35,000 per year.

It's important to realize that once your firm develops a reputation for coming in low on compensation, which could happen after only one instance, it can be difficult to recover. New hires and recent college graduates talk to each other, so please use caution if you're making what will be perceived as a lowball offer. Or, to avoid this problem altogether, make an offer that includes average or slightly above average base compensation with several incentive bonus opportunities added on. You'll likely find that candidates aren't necessarily interested in the highest base compensation offer, but instead want the best opportunity for future growth. As a final thought, I've observed that the price for top financial planning talent has skyrocketed in recent years, so if you're contemplating when to make your next hire, know that it will likely cost you more the longer you wait.

Navigating a Multiple Offer Environment

Today, more so than ever before, quality candidates are receiving multiple offers from multiple firms. If you find yourself in this competitive situation, here's what you can do to emerge as the frontrunner without giving away the farm.

Don't Focus Solely on Base Compensation—Be sure to highlight the *total* annual compensation that you're offering. It's important for a potential hire to visualize the firm's total outlay for compensation and benefits in order to understand their overall investment in her. Knowing this total amount is more important than simply being told how much will be direct deposited into a checking account every two weeks.

Reinforce Your Decision—It's important to inform your potential new hire that although there were other finalists in the running, she won out! This can reinforce certain impressions that the candidate may already have about you and your firm, such as candor, professionalism, and ethics—all of which lay the foundation for future loyalty. Furthermore, it gives the candidate a shot of confidence and provides insight into the appreciation and respect that you have for her.

Don't Lead on the Candidate—If you're only lukewarm about a candidate who has received multiple offers, be upfront and tell her. Don't be vague or lead her on, especially if she's shared her other offers and they appear stronger than yours. On the other hand, if you emphatically want to hire the candidate, tell her how excited you are about the prospect of her joining your firm. Remember, everyone likes to win and feel pursued from time to time.

By following the aforementioned guidelines, you can increase your chances of landing the next great hire without getting into a bidding war. Finally, and most importantly, remember that you have a compelling story to tell and your firm offers fabulous career growth opportunities. If the candidate cannot see that, it's probably not the right fit anyway.

CHAPTER 10

Training and Development

One of the common frustrations that I hear from existing employees when a new planner has been hired is something to the effect of, *"Management makes a hire without informing any of us, and now we have to take extra time above and beyond our current workload to train him!"* Undoubtedly, training a new planner can be time intensive, so establishing clear expectations up front with your current staff can help stave off some of this frustration. And just like with any large project, the work should be divided as equitably as possible to keep from overloading any one particular team member. Consider framing your training expectations as something like, *"I know you're currently overworked and that is not my intention, as this firm is committed to a work-life balance. I've made a key hire who can alleviate some of the bottlenecks we've been experiencing, thereby reducing your workload and stress. I'll need your assistance, which may mean additional short-term sacrifices, as we bring [planner name] up to speed. The sooner we can get [him/her] where [he/she] needs and wants to be, the sooner your work levels can return to normal. Thank you for your patience and understanding."*

Once the training process has formally begun, your primary focus should be educating the new planner on the intricacies of how your firm operates, regardless of her experience level. Training should not be viewed as an endeavor where you cross your fingers and hope something good comes of it. Instead, it should be seen as a chance to solidify your new planner's choice in selecting your firm to work for. Just as you strive to exceed the expectations of new clients that you bring on board, you should strive to do the same with new hires.

Unfortunately, this is easier said than done. From my experience, very few firms have adequate training programs in place, which sets the new planner up for potential failure. To provide additional context for this common challenge, see the communication excerpt below that I recently received from a frustrated new planner who decided to leave his firm.

"My position could best be described as an assistant to lead planners. As an associate planner, I did the typical back office work of preparing forms and researching cost basis, but it was the lead planners who had most of the interaction with clients. My interaction was limited to service work. I enjoy preparing financial plans and reports, however, I need client interaction related to the work I do, and I had very little opportunity for that.

In addition, I received no formal training for the tasks that I was expected to complete. I had to discover what those tasks were and then seek help in learning how to accomplish them. This was disconcerting and stressful to me, and unfair to my colleagues, who unexpectedly found themselves in the role of 'trainer,' with no prior notice from management, and with already full agendas of daily tasks."

This is not an isolated incident, and it's something that I encounter in financial planning firms nationwide. This message was particularly interesting, though, because it highlighted frustrations on both sides of the equation—the new hire as well as the current employees who were suddenly thrust into a training role they had not expected.

To add structure to your training program, and alleviate the common frustrations observed, be sure to implement the following 5-step action plan.

Step 1: Document Your Processes

Ideally, every process in your firm should be well-documented and easy to follow. This allows your new planner to learn your protocol efficiently, and also serves as a reference when existing team members have questions. Back when I worked as a financial planner and hired interns, I would send them our Processes and Procedures Manual that I had created, along with checklists, user guides to software programs, and custodian information. There was a clear expectation that these materials should be reviewed *before* the first day of work. (Rest assured that having an assortment of training materials is not "evil homework." If you've hired the right person, she will immerse herself in the materials that you've provided and will be excited to start using them.)

Step 2: Test Your Processes

Once you've documented all of your processes, spot-check them to ensure they're still accurate and don't need to be modified. Better yet, have one of your team members test a process who is otherwise unfamiliar with it. You may find that certain terms and abbreviations are well-understood by those with experience, but read like Greek to someone who is unfamiliar with the process.

Step 3: Create a Training Schedule

Be sure that you and your team members have set aside blocks of time each day to train your new planner. Realize that everyone will need to take a temporary step back from their daily activities in order to free up time for training, and don't underestimate the amount of training that will be required. As a rule of thumb, however long you think it will take to train a new planner, double it!

For a sample training schedule, see Appendix F.

Step 4: Let the Process Unfold

If you've made the right hire and instilled the proper culture, then your new planner should be able to navigate the training process with relative ease, and without fear of backlash if she needs to come to you with a question. Remember that it can be frustrating and stressful to learn a new process or use new software, let alone having to learn a whole new playbook. So be patient, have faith in your team members, and allow the process to unfold naturally.

Step 5: Reward Your Employees

Throughout the training process, you should be generous with praise and rewards for the efforts of your team members. If certain employees in particular have spent significant time training the new planner, then surprise them with a day or two off work, tickets to a local event, or some other means of demonstrating your appreciation.

Expectations for Your New Hire

To formalize your firm's training experience, I suggest providing guidelines like the ones below that clearly highlight your expectations for the new planner's level of competency at the three-month, six-month, one-year, two-year, and three-year marks. By communicating your current and future expectations, you're providing specific measurable items that must be achieved before advancing to more senior positions within your firm.

Note: For the example provided, client levels are Bronze, Silver, and Gold.

After 3 months, I expect you to:
- Become familiar with all office processes, procedures, and systems.
- Develop familiarity with all clients, strategic alliances, and software programs.
- Respond to Bronze client service requests to begin developing rapport.
- Be able to communicate firm investment philosophies and planning processes to clients and prospects.
- Join professional associations such as FPA, NAPFA, AICPA, SFSP, IMCA.
- Recognize your strengths and identify areas in need of further improvement.

After 6 months, I expect you to:

- Be comfortable talking with clients and become the primary contact for Bronze clients.
- Be the secondary contact for Silver and Gold clients.
- Become the in-house expert on _____ financial planning software, _____ custodian platform, and _____ asset management software.
- Participate in, and contribute to, client meetings.
- Take the lead on certain projects delegated by senior staff members.
- Pass licensing exams for Series 7, 65, 66.

After 1 year, I expect you to:

- Manage all aspects of the financial planning process, including preliminary analysis, scenario creation, and planning deliverables.
- Begin leading data gathering/discovery meetings.
- Develop a minimum of _____ strategic alliances through your own networking and marketing efforts.
- Bring in a minimum of _____ Bronze and Silver clients to our firm through your own networking and marketing efforts.
- Secure a position on a professional association committee or board.
- Pass the CFP® Certification Exam.
- Have an "owner" mentality and take a proactive approach to client services.

After 2 years, I expect you to:

- Lead staff meetings and financial planning brainstorming sessions.
- Present new ideas to our firm for marketing, technology, and planning deliverables.

- Be the primary contact for Bronze and Silver clients.
- Develop a minimum of _____ strategic alliances through your own networking and marketing efforts.
- Bring in a minimum of _____ Bronze and Silver clients to our firm through your own networking and marketing efforts.
- Be comfortable talking with media and responding to inquiries where appropriate.
- Attend conferences and report back on best practices and ideas that our firm should consider implementing.

After 3 years, I expect you to:
- Begin leading financial planning presentations and implementation meetings.
- Be the primary contact for all strategic alliances.
- Bring in a minimum of _____ Silver and Gold clients to our firm through your own networking and marketing efforts.
- Be the primary contact for Bronze, Silver, and Gold clients.
- Interview, hire, and manage interns.
- Contribute to our firm's marketing efforts through networking, article writing, newsletter content development, and speaking engagements.
- Attend conferences and network with industry leaders.

In addition to these measurable items, I also encourage both firm owners and new planners to commit to the pledges provided on the following pages. The owner's pledge demonstrates a continued interest in seeing each new planner succeed. The new planner's pledge reinforces a willingness to be coached and mentored in order to develop into the best planner possible.

The Team Member Pledge for Owners

- I will inform our new planners of future business plans, as they might offer valuable and interesting input. I realize that they will be more committed to our firm and its long-term success if they are part of the conversation.
- I will ensure that our new planners have the best equipment available and the most up-to-date software so that our efficiency doesn't suffer.
- I will remember what I said during the interview and hiring process regarding our new planners' roles, responsibilities, and career path. I will follow through as promised as long as they are delivering as expected.
- I will provide our new planners with positive reinforcement in addition to constructive criticism.
- I will keep our new planners informed as to whether or not they are meeting expectations.
- I will spend time mentoring our new planners, show confidence in them, exhibit patience, and view them as the professionals they are.
- I will let our new planners communicate with clients and will consider letting them hone their skills by presenting the analysis they performed.
- I will take a genuine interest in learning about our new planners' interests and family lives. I understand that family always wins!
- I will consider adjusting the culture and work environment of our firm as needed to accommodate our new planners, and to ensure they are satisfied and enjoy coming to work. I realize that if I don't, another firm surely will.

- I will not involve new planners in disputes between partners or senior staff members and force them to choose sides.
- I will not take out any personal feelings of frustration or anger on our new planners at any time.

The Team Member Pledge for New Planners

- I will realize that other job opportunities may be presented to me by competing firms, but I am committed to growing within our firm and hustling every day to help our team succeed.
- I will strive to always increase my level of expertise and professionalism so that I can perform well beyond my years.
- I will go above and beyond the minimum requirements for my position and all tasks delegated to me in an effort to help our firm succeed.
- I will work hard to show the owner that I'm serious about developing as a financial planner, and I will strive to reduce the risks associated with hiring and mentoring me.
- I will fix mistakes as they are brought to my attention so the owner does not have to repeatedly provide the same instruction.
- I will be humble and respectful in any ideas that I provide to the owner, especially if they are unsolicited.
- I will understand that the owner's career path is different than mine, and I might not succeed in the profession if not for the opportunity that I've been provided.
- I will never be satisfied with the status quo and I will always push to better myself, our firm, and our service to clients.

- I will ask the owner, on a regular basis, how I am progressing, how I can improve, and if there are more complicated tasks that I can work on to better assist the firm.
- I will inform the owner of any career doubts that I might be having, plans to resign, or the need to take extended time off so that necessary arrangements can be made so the firm is not negatively impacted.
- I will be sensitive to the fact that I am not the owner, and that I do not have the final say, even if I disagree with the owner's decision.

CHAPTER 11

Positioning New Hires for Success

One of the primary reasons that a firm owner hires a new planner is to free up her time to perform the higher-level revenue producing tasks that her more experienced skill set is suited for, such as working with high net worth clients and securing new clients. Therefore, it's imperative that your new planner begins working with your existing clients as soon as she's ready. To achieve this, here are the steps that your firm should take to introduce, integrate, and effectively position your new planner within your firm.

Add to Website and Phone Tree—Post your new planner's photo and biography on your website to reinforce to clients and prospects that she's an integral part of your team.

Send a Welcome Letter—Introduce your new hire to your clients, colleagues, and strategic alliances by sending a welcome letter. This can be part of your regular client touches, but preferably it would be a standalone correspondence to promote its importance. Be sure to highlight the new planner's credentials, education, and experience, and describe why you hired her and how she will be helping your clients. Also include the planner's business card if you're sending a physical letter. *For a sample welcome letter, see Appendix G.*

Have the Planner Reply to Client Inquiries—Have your new planner respond to client voicemails and correspondence to refine her communication skills and train clients that they don't have to contact you for everything! Initially you'll have to work alongside your new planner to achieve this, but clients will slowly be trained to go to her first, and then she will escalate to you when necessary.

Have the Planner Confirm Upcoming Meetings—Consider having your new planner attend all of your client meetings for the first several weeks. Prior to each meeting, have the planner contact the client to confirm the appointment and ask if there are any items that should be added to the meeting agenda.

Script suggestion: *"Hello [client name], this is [planner's name] and I'm working with [firm owner's name] preparing for your upcoming meeting on [day of week]. I wanted to confirm that this [day of week] at [time of day] still works for you and [spouse's name]? ...... Okay, great! We have several items that we want to go over with you, but do you have anything specific that you would like to add to the agenda? ...... Okay, I'll make sure we're prepared to discuss that. I look forward to meeting you in person! See you on [day of week]."*

Have the Planner Participate in Client Meetings—Spend the first few moments of each meeting introducing the new planner and discussing her credentials and role within the firm. Then you can present the financial plan to the client as usual, while the new planner takes notes. Throughout the meeting, ask the new planner a few basic questions so she can answer in front of the client. This empowers the new planner and reinforces that she's an integral part of your team.

Have the Planner Follow up with Clients—After each client meeting, carefully review the notes that the new planner took, and ask her what she learned during the meeting. This stimulates discussion and promotes growth opportunities for both you and the planner. Afterwards, have the new planner send a meeting summary to the client.

Script suggestion: *"Hello [client name], it was great to finally meet you and [spouse's name] in person! I have attached the notes that we took during your meeting. Please review them to make sure that we've captured everything correctly, and let us know if any changes are needed. Also, I've attached the pre-filled paperwork for the [insert activity, e.g. Roth conversion, open a brokerage account, etc.] that we discussed. Please sign and return at your convenience, and call me with any questions. We hope you have a great day!"*

After several weeks have passed, I recommend evaluating the new planner's overall integration with your firm to look for any potential red flags. Use the following chart to assist you in gauging how well she's been acclimating to your firm and how your existing team members have been accepting her. If you notice that any of the warning signals apply, have a frank discussion with the new planner to get to the heart of the problem and craft a solution.

Acceptance Signals	Warning Signals
Team members remain friendly with the new planner after the "honeymoon period" ends.	Team members avoid the new planner whenever possible.
The new planner's "good" ideas are accepted with enthusiasm.	All of the new planner's ideas are rejected without evaluation.
The new planner's "poor" ideas are (respectfully) declined with feedback as to why they weren't implemented.	Team members support "poor" ideas in an attempt to "set up" the new planner for failure.
Other team members seek information and ideas from the new planner.	No one seeks input from the new planner. His/her ideas and opinions are not valued.
The new planner is included in organizational functions as appropriate.	The new planner is left out of organizational functions.
The new planner is seen as "one of us."	The new planner is still seen as an outsider.

Source: Oregon State University: Integrating New Employees to the Workplace

What New Planners Wish They Could Tell Their Bosses

Once the training process is complete, your work as firm owner is far from over. It's now your job to foster a culture of collaboration, where your new planner feels valued and respected. Most firm owners tend to view their companies as perfect tens, far removed from the common problems that hinder their competitors. But when I follow up with new planners several months after they've been hired, I often receive a lot of interesting feedback that firm owners would be surprised by. Here I'll share the top five comments that I commonly receive from new planners, and the takeaway for firm owners.

- Planner comment: *"The expectations here are not clear and I have no way to tell if I'm measuring up."*

  Employer takeaway: Develop clear expectations prior to hiring and make sure that you communicate them early and often throughout the training process. Avoid vague statements such as, "Get this work done as fast as possible," and, "Just do what I do." Instead, be specific, such as, "Become the in-house Moneytree expert within six months," or, "Develop two new strategic alliance referral sources this month."

- Planner comment: *"I was told to explore, be creative, and try new things to develop my own style, but what the owner really meant was, 'You'd better do it my way.'"*

  Employer takeaway: If you've hired the best and brightest candidate, putting the reins on her creativity is short-changing your firm's investment in her and stunting your growth. If your intention is truly to "have it done your way," then frame it as, "Do it my way until you've mastered it, then you can improvise."

- Planner comment: *"My supervisors are not approachable. They're busy and become visibly frustrated when I ask a question. When I do get a chance to speak with them, they answer my question with a question or belittle me because I don't know something they feel that I should."*

Employer takeaway: If your firm has experienced high turnover and employee dissatisfaction, being unapproachable could be one of the root causes. Gen Y planners are looking for a collaborative work atmosphere. If they don't feel like they're receiving basic guidance and feedback, they will take the knowledge that you've imparted on them and leave to join the competition.

- Planner comment: *"I'm not performing the role that I was hired for. I feel underutilized and unchallenged, and my employer thinks that 'challenging me' means giving me more daily tasks to complete."*

Employer takeaway: New planners want challenging work, but this doesn't necessarily mean *more* work. They want assignments that challenge them to learn something new and expand their skills. As an owner, realize that it's easy for a planner to fall into a rut performing the same tasks for the same clients every day.

- Planner comment: *"The mentoring, resources, and camaraderie that I need to grow and succeed doesn't currently exist."*

Employer takeaway: Periodically ask your planners if they have the tools and resources needed to successfully serve clients. A simple check-in from time to time to validate their existence and contributions to your firm is a powerful tool that costs nothing. Camaraderie cannot be forced, but owners leading small firms can encourage planners to become involved in networking groups which benefit both them and the firm.

CHAPTER 12

---◦·◦---

How to Handle Underperformers

A t some point in your firm's lifecycle, you will encounter financial planners who underperform. Although underperformance comes in various shapes and sizes, it's most commonly considered an inability to complete job-specific tasks quickly and accurately. If not addressed properly, underperformers can wreak havoc on your firm's work flow and profitability. The following "dos and don'ts" are meant to guide you towards bringing an underperforming planner back up to the service standards that you're accustomed to.

Do: Establish performance goals jointly.

I find that firm owners often do a poor job communicating their expectations to new planners, and these planners go on to become underperformers months later. It's not entirely the planner's fault, since she can't be expected to meet or exceed expectations that you failed to verbalize. To remedy this common problem, be sure to set specific goals and reasonable timeframes. As the leader of your firm, it's your responsibility to create these expectations initially—preferably in writing—and then build upon them collaboratively with your new planner so that she buys in to your vision. This approach will also assist you when it comes time to do an annual review, because it will allow you to take an objective approach by revisiting the document that you and the planner developed together.

Don't: Focus exclusively on the negatives.

When a planner on your team is struggling, it's your job to look for ways to boost his or her confidence. Maybe it's a compliment on something that's being done well— even if it's just one thing! Realistically, if you cannot find a single thing that the planner is doing well, then you should never hire again without professional assistance. If the planner that you hired has any awareness whatsoever, he or she is probably already aware that your expectations are not being met. Take this opportunity to ask questions to find the cause of the downturn and to determine if it's temporary. Use the conversation as a chance to build confidence and ignite the planner's desire to succeed.

Do: Offer to provide additional training and resources.

By this point, you've probably already invested a great deal of time and resources into the planner's career, and you should be willing to exhaust all options prior to pulling the plug. Maybe the solution is as straightforward as additional training in something like time management, efficiency, listening, professionalism, or communication. Consider bringing in a coach or consultant who can assist with instruction and accountability, and can also provide objective insight into the planner's progress and likely future outcome. Furthermore, if the underperformance is corrected, these steps that you took will instill a great sense of loyalty in the planner.

Don't: Shift work to other team members.

I encourage firm owners to deal with underperformers directly, and to not be lured into having other team members pick up the slack. Often times a firm owner will put off having a difficult conversation about a planner's underperformance "until it's a better time," and in the meantime, the underperformer's workload is pushed onto others. Having your high performers occasionally pick up the slack is one thing, but you endanger losing them if it continues for too long. You don't want to send the wrong message to your high performers that they will be punished by having to shoulder more of the workload because you can count on them.

Do: Ask for input on what you might be missing.

Consider reaching out to peers, study groups, and colleagues from the planner's generation to gain their perspective on why he or she may be underperforming. For example, if your underperformer is from Gen Y, then reach out to a member of FPA NexGen or NAPFA Genesis. After some due diligence on your part, you may find that you simply aren't as good at managing as you thought, and your underperforming planner is just the first of more to come. Or you may discover that you made a bad hire, or your expectations are indeed too lofty. Either way, surround yourself with people who will be honest with you so that you can accurately diagnose the problem and then work to correct it.

Don't: Ask underperformers to train their replacements.

Training is not what most independent financial planning firms are known for, hence one of the reasons that new hires struggle. So if a planner is underperforming, having him or her train a replacement will only perpetuate the problem. Before long you'll be going through the same hiring and firing process all over again. Instead, think about what in the process went wrong, and how it can be corrected before your next hire.

If you've already tried the aforementioned strategies and you're still not able to secure the outcome that you had hoped for, then parting ways may be your only remaining option. Terminating an employee can be one of the most nerve-wracking and difficult experiences that an owner has to face. But when a team member is underperforming, the effects can ripple through the entire firm and cause long-term damage. For this reason, if you've exhausted all other options and deemed it necessary to terminate an employee, follow these guidelines for the conversation and subsequent follow up.

Deliver the News in Person—Avoid terminating an employee via phone, email, or text. If possible, meet in a neutral place like a conference room (not your private office), and bring a witness, whether it's a staff manager, HR representative, or senior employee, to validate what was said in the meeting.

Be Direct at the Onset of the Meeting—Make it clear to the employee at the beginning of the meeting that he or she is being terminated. Try to keep the conversation as positive and neutral as possible, but make sure the employee understands this is not a negotiation or mere "wake up call."

Create a Script—Although you don't want to appear rehearsed or like you're reading from a notecard, creating a script ahead of time will ensure that you deliver the correct message and steer clear of any legal hurdles. After checking with your specific state regulations, compliance requirements, and HR department, consider something to the effect of, *"Thanks for meeting with me. I think you know what we are here to discuss, but if not, as we've alluded to over the last several months, you have not been able to meet the goals that we have jointly set for you here at our company. Because of this, we are terminating your employment as we specified that we would during our last meeting. We appreciate your contribution to our firm and we will offer you the following severance package while you look for a new position."*

Allow for Self-Reflection—Ask yourself what you could have done differently in the months leading up to the eventual termination. A well-known and successful firm owner in South Carolina once said, "If it doesn't work out with an employee, it's mostly my fault." Even though this sentiment was not popular with some of her peers, it's quite revealing about her management style and firm culture. Realistically, though, this is a foreign concept to many firm owners who prefer not to self-reflect and take ownership of the fact that they may be to blame. If your firm has experienced frequent turnover, then the constant in the situation is you, and perhaps a change in your management style is warranted.

CHAPTER 13

Succession Planning

It's true that we are a graying profession, and there's a great deal of debate about the best way to go about alleviating the problem of the next generation continuing the work that the founding generation has started. I find that when tackling their succession challenges, most firm owners try to find successors just like themselves to take over their businesses. So they seek out Type A, entrepreneurial, extroverted, sales oriented candidates. This may seem like a logical approach because, after all, these are valuable traits that the founder herself possesses. But they are not necessarily the most important qualities that a successor needs in order to ensure a firm's continued success. Instead, I encourage owners to find successor candidates who are innovative, have an innate sense of urgency, and are good at follow through. Candidates that I have placed over the years who possess these three qualities have gone on to become the most successful firm owners due to the unique leadership applications discussed below.

- **Being an Innovator**—The financial planning profession has evolved immensely over the last few years, and the firms that continue to adapt in the future will thrive.

Sure, there are many firms that are practicing the same business model as they did ten years ago, but they are in survive versus thrive mode. Whoever is going to lead your firm in the future must be comfortable taking risks and trying new things. The challenges that your firm will face over the next thirty years will be far different than the challenges that you faced over the previous thirty, and your successor needs to realize this.

When reviewing successor candidates, look for someone who has taken a risk in her past, even if that risk ultimately proved to be unsuccessful. While it's human nature to want to focus on our successes, we learn much more by reflecting on our defeats. If you're having trouble finding such a candidate, consider attending an FPA Retreat, where you'll be surrounded by hundreds of innovators in the financial planning profession.

- **Having a Sense of Urgency**—Your successor's mindset should be, "If I don't get this done for [insert name] by [insert date], it will be detrimental to the business." The importance of this quality cannot be underestimated, as the service level that financial planning firms provide—and that clients demand—continues to increase. With this extra workload, a candidate with a sense of urgency will be well-positioned for success. Urgency breeds initiative, and there are several ways to screen for this characteristic, such as by asking, "Can you tell me about a time where you had to delay a deliverable?" (Notably, though, a candidate could prepare for this type of question, so it might give you a false sense of her urgency.) Consider also building competing deadlines into your screening process to see if the candidate meets them.

Keep in mind, there is a fine line between getting work done efficiently and accurately, and doing so in a manner that induces anxiety and leads to burnout. A candidate with leadership qualities will be aware of this, and will know how to manage it effectively for herself and the team members that she supervises.

- **The Ability to Follow Through**—Often found alongside high integrity, follow through is simply the art of doing what you say you're going to do. Unfortunately, this is becoming an increasingly rare characteristic among all generations. As a society, it's become commonplace to brush off upholding a commitment by simply saying we're "too busy." Technology has created efficiencies in the workplace, but it has also created additional demands and distractions for our time, leading us to overpromise and underdeliver.

    Identifying candidates who are strong in follow through is difficult because every candidate will want you to believe that they possess this quality. To effectively screen for it, look for candidates who specify their goals in writing or in a public format. The main reason that people don't specify goals or share them with others is because they don't want to deal with the fallout if they're not completed. Conversely, those who are willing to state their concrete goals are more likely to be the ones who will follow through to achieve them.

These qualities may seem obvious, but many candidates lack these simple attributes, and few will have all three. If you're seeking a potential successor, I encourage you to resist the urge to try to find an exact replica of yourself. Instead, explore candidates who may be wired a little differently, even if it means searching outside the profession.

Preparing Your Business for a Successor

To provide your successor with the best possible chance to succeed, it's necessary to consider integration in each of the following three areas of your business: Client service, business management, and new business development. Recognize that the dynamics will be different depending on whether you've selected an internal or external successor, as explained below.

- ### Client Service

Because financial planning is primarily a relationship-based business, telling your clients that you'll no longer be their primary planner is a delicate process. The reality is that the value of a succession planning transaction is largely based on how many first-generation clients will be retained once the original firm owner has departed. Forward thinking firms will be deliberate about the client transition process and will begin conditioning clients for such a change early on.

Internal Successor: If you've selected an internal successor, the positioning is much more about getting clients to recognize that your former protégé is now your equal. Convincing clients to overcome their recency bias can be difficult, since they've probably always known your successor as the "second-chair planner" in their meetings. However, if your clients implicitly trust you, and you tell them that your successor is taking over for you, then most should in turn be comfortable with your decision. After all, they too have likely witnessed your successor's growth before their own eyes.

External Successor: For an external successor, it's imperative that you both attend at least a handful of meetings together for each client. Depending on your firm's service model, this could take several months to several years. When you've reached the point where your successor can take over as the lead planner for a particular client, have her write a one-page brief describing the client's family, their unique financial planning issues, and the approach to facing those issues moving forward. These briefs are meant to provide you with a level of comfort before completing each client transition.

- **Business Management**

Having technical expertise and command of each client's financial situation will not be sufficient if your firm is otherwise mismanaged from a strategic planning standpoint. Sound business management is essential to your firm's survival after you've left.

Internal Successor: Begin involving your successor in the firm's financial and strategic planning decisions as early as possible. Educate her on your decision-making process and the financial guidelines that you use to manage the business, and serve as a mentor as she begins to manage staff. If you're unwilling to share your firm's financials for fear of retribution once your successor realizes the level of income that you're earning, then you may need to reconsider your choice of successor altogether.

External Successor: The hurdle that an external successor faces is garnering acceptance from the existing team. If not communicated properly, the team members who were passed over as successor will resent—and possibly try to sabotage—the new arrival's transition. As firm owner, sharing with your team something to the effect of, "I was too caught up in building the business and did a poor job developing our existing team members to take over," will go a long way towards reducing contempt for an outsider who will most likely implement changes once her tenure begins.

- **New Business Development**

Firms that are well established typically don't need a "pound the pavement" type of successor, mainly because the founder already did that. Instead, these firms need a successor who will take care of the existing client relationships and strategic alliances at such a high level that they will refer everyone they know.

Internal Successor: Consider taking your successor with you on all strategic alliance meetings for as many months or years as needed so she can see firsthand what it takes for these referral sources to build up enough trust to begin referring clients. This also gives your successor a small glimpse at what you had to go through when you started your firm years ago. While it's important that you expose your successor to your style and methods, do not expect her to continue them verbatim. Before the succession is complete, make sure that your successor has a strategy as to which organizations and associations she plans to actively participate in to keep the firm engaged with prospective clients. For the most part, boards and charities are saturated with "financial advisors," so your candidate should instead consider a Blue Ocean such as targeting the next generation of entrepreneurs through the Young Entrepreneur Council, FoundersCard, Startup Grind, and others.

External Successor: While it's common for an external successor to have a pool of clients to bring to your firm, you need to examine if the clients are a good fit for your firm's overall vision. A sudden influx of new clients can seem like a panacea, but onboarding and integrating clients into your service model can be laborious and put a strain on already limited resources during a transition. If your successor will be bringing in new clients who you have deemed to not be a good fit, be wary of making special exceptions because "revenue is revenue." If you're not careful, your firm will have a subset of clients with a different pricing and service model that you never intended to have in the first place.

Implementing Your Succession Plan

Once you've determined *who*, it's time to move on to *how*. It's your job as founder to groom your chosen successor into who you know she can become, and what your firm needs to succeed when you step aside. To achieve this, and thereby extract as much value as possible from your life's work, follow these developmental tips.

Become a "Hyper" Mentor—It's your job to ensure that you've transferred all of your knowledge, skills, and abilities to your successor. This can best be accomplished through a mentoring relationship on steroids. There should be a plethora of scheduled meetings, late night phone calls, and weekend get-togethers to increase your successor's absorption of your "data dump." Once you're confident that your successor's technical skills are sound, switch your focus to the softer skills such as empathy, awareness, patience, and the art of sequencing questions to clients and staff to lead conversations where you want them to go.

Make Decisions Together—Develop guidelines on joint decision-making metrics and a reasonable timeline to implement them. Much of this will depend on the terms of the succession plan that you've already agreed to, but the basic idea is to make joint decisions with your successor for a certain period of time, and then switch sole decision-making authority over to your successor afterwards.

Also, be sensitive to the potential awkwardness that may ensue if you're required to stay with the firm after you've handed over the keys. From the successor's perspective, this is like purchasing a new home and moving in while the original owner is still occupying one of the bedrooms! Not exactly desirable for the successor.

Do a CEO Test Run—Put your successor on the hot seat for a trial run to see if any developmental areas are in need of further mentoring. Resist the urge to throw out a lifeline if you observe your successor struggling a bit. Remember, you too had a learning curve and the purpose of this test run is an honest assessment of your successor's ability to identify problems and determine how best to resolve them. Pay special attention to how your successor handles staffing and HR issues. These serve as great measures of patience, steadfastness, and resilience, which are all qualities a good CEO must possess.

Communicating the Process and Timeline

It's important for both the founder and successor to keep staff informed throughout the succession process in order to ensure a smooth transition. Since not everyone is privy to all of the details, it's your responsibility to communicate the succession process effectively and keep your staff up to date on pertinent information. Avoid statements like, "We are entering into a succession arrangement, so be prepared for some changes." Instead, say something like, "We are entering into a succession arrangement because _____. The transition will begin by _____, and should take _____ months to complete. Here is what you can expect, and what we will need from you during this time: _____." While it may be obvious how the succession will benefit you as the owner, frame it so that your staff sees how it will serve as a growth opportunity for them, as well.

Remember that most people don't like surprises, especially when their careers and livelihoods are affected. Because of this, it's critical that both you and your successor communicate any potential culture of developmental changes early and often. Once you've communicated the succession process in detail, be certain that you're physically present and available to answer any questions that your staff may have.

As the succession process nears completion, encourage your successor to resist the urge to scale back or eliminate training and professional development programs in an effort to make the first-year financials look more attractive. Rather than cutting programs and benefits, your successor should instead be focusing on tying employee compensation to incentives designed to retain clients, continue momentum, learn new systems, and complete the integration process. Above all else, remember that your firm's greatest asset is its human capital. Retaining employees and keeping them motivated and excited to come to work is the only way that a financial planning firm can survive. Although there is no silver bullet when it comes to ensuring employees will stay with your firm after a succession, the strategies outlined in this chapter will go a long way towards shaping an attractive culture that increases employee morale and cultivates a positive work environment.

APPENDIX A

Sample Job Description

We are seeking an Associate Financial Planner for our fee-only wealth management firm in Anytown, USA. We are interested in you if you're a recent graduate from a CFP® Board Registered Program who desires a small firm environment; wants to be involved in all aspects of the business, learning and shaping the way we care for our clients; wants to learn from three industry veterans; and is excited to work your way up our advisory career ladder. Candidates that fit into our firm culture will desire to be in a small independent RIA firm environment acting in a fiduciary capacity, and will embrace technology and working in a team setting.

<u>Position Overview</u>

This is a professional position that will initially support the firm's three Partners directly in managing existing and new client relationships. You will be expected to assist in various projects including portfolio reviews and preparing financial projections using Microsoft Excel spreadsheets and MoneyGuidePro financial planning software. Thorough computer skills are essential, with a particularly strong understanding of Excel. A working knowledge of portfolio allocation, investment management, and general financial planning is expected. The Partners are available to provide mentoring and big picture direction, but you must have the ability to utilize critical thinking skills, work independently, and anticipate firm needs and client questions.

Initial Areas of Responsibility:

- Assist Partners in preparing for and conducting client meetings and regularly monitor clients' financial situations with attention to detail and accuracy.
- Involvement in all aspects of pre-client meeting activities, such as gathering data, preparing agendas, and assisting with client paperwork and asset allocations. You will also be responsible for post-client meeting activities, such as developing meeting summaries, performing financial situation analyses, and coordinating planning implementation with outside professionals.
- Work with MoneyGuidePro, PortfolioCenter (PMS), Tamarac Rebalancer, Tamarac Advisor View, and Tamarac CRM (Microsoft Dynamics CRM).
- Interact with clients over the phone and in-person.

Potential Future Areas of Responsibility:

- Assist with trading and rebalancing client investment accounts.
- Deliver multidisciplinary financial planning advice for high net worth clientele independently.
- Develop and manage ongoing client relationships independently.
- Present 401(k) plan participant group education sessions.

- Delegate appropriate tasks to supporting team members.
- Provide input on strategic plan and overall direction of the firm.

Qualifications:
- Organized, with a strong attention to detail.
- B.A. or B.S. degree from a CFP® Board Registered Program.
- Strong financial and analytical skills.
- Strong persuasive and interpersonal skills.
- Ability to identify, meet, and follow through with client needs and requirements.
- Must be a self-starter, problem solver, and a goal-oriented team player with a "no job is beneath me" attitude.
- Ability to work independently and keep Partners aware of progress and challenges.
- Show curiosity and confidence when dealing with clients and Partners.

Benefits:
- Qualifies for the CFP® Board apprenticeship two-year work experience requirement
- Competitive salary with performance-based pay program
- 401(k) with company match
- Group health insurance
- Professional development budget for CEs, conferences, and training
- Paid professional dues
- Mentorship and learning opportunities
- Company paid parking

APPENDIX B
Candidate Rejection Letter

Subject: Candidacy Status with [Firm Name]

Dear [Candidate's Name]:

Thank you for expressing interest in employment at [Firm Name], and particularly the position of [Job Title]. We have appreciated the opportunity to review your background. At this time, we would like to inform you that we have identified other candidates whose qualifications and experience are a better fit for this position. We will keep your information on file and may contact you in the future if other job openings match your profile.

We wish you the best in your job search.

Sincerely,

[Your Name]

APPENDIX C

Sample Interview Agenda

Note: The following agenda assumes a remote candidate visiting a firm for her final interview.

9:00 A.M. — Interview

- Have the candidate summarize her expectations of a role with your firm, and then discuss your expectations of the candidate.
- Discuss strategic planning and ask the candidate how she would have responded to certain situations that lead planners at your firm had to recently address.
- Show the candidate how to navigate a software program employed by your firm, then move on to a different subject, and a few minutes later come back to the software program and ask the candidate to recall your instructions.

10:30 A.M. — Observe Associate Planners

- Have various associate planners show the candidate their daily work activities and have them review procedures, account maintenance, meeting preparation, software programs, and client communication.

- Ensure that the candidate has a glimpse of what tasks she would be performing on a daily basis, who she would be working with, and the environment where she would be working.

11:30 A.M. — Lunch

- Preferably, lunch would be with associate planners exclusively.
- Allow the candidate and associate planners to have a frank discussion about the firm and its culture.

1:30 P.M. — Observe Lead Planners

- Have various lead planners show the candidate their daily work activities and have them review the client meeting process.
- Demonstrate to the candidate how the associate planner and lead planner work together to service clients.

Break

3:00 P.M. — Observe Support Staff

- Begin by asking the candidate to explain a few of the processes and procedures that she observed earlier in the day. (The goal is to ensure that the candidate's follow through and attention to detail are at the level required for the position.)
- Conclude by having the remaining office staff demonstrate any pertinent items not previously discussed.

5:30 P.M. — Dinner

- Have team members take the candidate to dinner to enjoy a more relaxed environment.
- Try to gain an understanding of the candidate's passions, ethics, morals, and overall demeanor.

APPENDIX D

Compensation Summary

Example 1

Position Compensation:
- Base compensation of $52,500 per year, paid bi-weekly.
- Business development incentive: You will receive 15% of all first-year revenue sourced directly by you.
- Upon passing the CFP® Certification Exam, you will be eligible for a one-time bonus of $2,500. Additionally, your CFP® license is required to advance on our advisory career ladder, which has the opportunity to lead to base compensation increases and additional business development incentives.

Benefits:
- Firm benefits are provided via our HSA plan, as outlined in the attached information. Our benefits consultant will assist you in selecting the appropriate plan to meet your needs.
- Employees are responsible for paying their own individual premium costs for the HSA plan. The firm will make a quarterly contribution in the amount of $675 to your selected HSA plan.

- Should you opt out of the HSA plan, 80% of the total contribution by our firm ($2,160 annually) is available for you to pay fees associated with another benefit plan. Proof of enrollment and coverage will be required, and payments will be made quarterly to you via payroll contributions.
- Approximately nine paid holidays per year, as outlined in the attached holiday schedule.
- Two weeks annual paid vacation for years one through five; three weeks for years six through ten; and four weeks thereafter.

Example 2

Your compensation and benefits package includes:
- Base compensation: $2,500 per month
- Incentive compensation: 25% of financial planning fees paid by your clients. (Approximately $10,000 to $15,000 paid out quarterly.)
- Firm profitability bonus: 1% of annual firm revenue if pre-specified performance targets are met.
- Achievement bonus: $2,000 paid upon successfully passing the CFP® Certification Exam.
- Retirement plan: Roth 401(k) with 4% company match.
- Medical benefits: 50% premiums paid, with an additional $3,450 bonus paid in Q1 directly into your HSA.
- Conferences and training: To be determined based on approval.
- Paid time off: Ten days annually for your first two years of employment. See policy and terms.
- Holidays: New Year's Day, Good Friday, Memorial Day, Independence Day, Labor Day, Thanksgiving, the day

after Thanksgiving, Christmas Day, and the day after Christmas.
- Estimated total compensation for first year of employment: $50,450

Example 3

Your compensation and benefits package includes:
- Base compensation: $3,300 per month
- Signing bonus: $2,500
- Exam and licensing fees: Series 66 exam and CFP® Certification Exam licensing costs will be fully reimbursed.
- Achievement bonus: $600 paid upon successfully passing the Series 66 exam.
- Achievement bonus: $1,800 paid upon successfully passing the CFP® Certification Exam.
- Medical benefits: The firm will pay 100% of an HSA-based health insurance plan.
- Vacation: Two weeks paid vacation for first twelve months of employment.
- Paid holidays: New Year's Day, Memorial Day, Independence Day, Labor Day, Thanksgiving, the day after Thanksgiving, Christmas Day, and the day after Christmas if Christmas falls on a Thursday.
- Membership and dues: The firm will pay your CFP® Certification dues, and will provide membership to the Financial Planning Association.
- Total annual compensation: $44,500

APPENDIX E

Offer Letter

Subject: [Job Title] with [Firm Name]

Dear [Candidate's Name]:

On behalf of [Firm Name], it's our pleasure to extend to you this offer of employment for [Job Title].

Your compensation and benefits package includes:
- **Base salary:** $50,000 per year, paid bi-weekly.
- **Incentive bonus:** 1% of annual firm revenue, payable twice per year by January 31 and July 31. Please note that you must be an employee of the firm on the last day of the calculation period (June 30 and December 31) to receive this incentive bonus. The first bonus will be pro-rated based on start date.
- **Retirement plan contribution:** Minimum 3% of compensation. You will be eligible to participate in the [Retirement Plan Name] after six months of employment. The [Retirement Plan Name] has a 4-year vesting schedule of 25% per year.
- **Medical insurance:** The firm will pay 50% of your insurance premium, subject to a maximum amount of

$300 per month. Please note that because you will need to acquire an individual policy, you must pay the premiums yourself, and the firm contributions will be paid as additional income to you. Both you and the firm will pay taxes on this amount, and it will be included in your total compensation for purposes of calculating your annual [Retirement Plan Name] contribution.

- **Vacation:** 3 weeks
- **NAPFA membership:** $600
- **CFP® Certification licensing:** $355
- **Conference/Continuing education allowance:** $1,000
- **Holidays:** New Year's Day, President's Day, Good Friday, Memorial Day, Independence Day, Labor Day, Thanksgiving, and Christmas Day

Estimated total annual compensation: $63,000

Performance and compensation will be reviewed in December of [current year] and annually thereafter.

Our firm is dedicated to serving our clients, hiring the best people, and helping you make the most of your talents. We are looking forward to having you join our team. Please feel free to call me if you have any questions about our offer.

Sincerely,

[Your Name]

Please indicate your acceptance of this offer by signing below and returning it via email or mail to [Firm Name] by [date].

- -

I have read this letter and understand and accept its terms. I understand that I will be required to sign a non-disclosure, non-solicitation, and non-compete agreement for consideration of employment at [Firm Name]. I also understand that this offer is contingent on a successful background, credit, and reference check.

[Candidate Name]: _____

Date: _____

APPENDIX F

Sample Training Schedule

Note: The following training schedule is for a new hire's first day of work.

9:00 A.M. — Meet the Staff

- Welcome to the firm.
- Provide welcome kit with branded items such as shirt, hat, backpack, and umbrella.
- Provide overview of training schedule.
- Discuss job duties, responsibilities, and performance expectations.
- Provide organizational chart and reporting structure.
- Provide office tour and introduce team members.
- Point person: Office manager

9:30 A.M. — Discuss New Hire Onboarding

- Discuss onboarding documents including I-9, W-4 (and state withholding if applicable), direct deposit paperwork, W-2 consent, and benefits information.
- Present the employee handbook with signed acknowledgement of receipt.

- Review work station area, computer hardware, and other equipment provided.
- Point person: Office manager

10:00 A.M. — Introduce CRM Program

- Systems training: Introduce the firm's CRM program such as Redtail, Junxure, Tamarac, or Salesforce.
- Point person: Associate planner

11:30 A.M. — Lunch with Team

1:00 P.M. — Introduce Financial Planning Software

- Systems training: Introduce the firm's financial planning software such as Moneytree, MoneyGuidePro, eMoney, or NaviPlan.
- Point person: Associate planner

Break

3:00 P.M. — Introduce Client Meeting Process

- Familiarize the new hire with the firm's meeting process for existing and prospective clients.
- Point person: Lead planner

5:00 P.M. — Dinner

- Dinner with direct supervisor to discuss ongoing training program.

APPENDIX G

Welcome Letter

Subject: Here We Grow Again!

Dear Clients, Friends, and Colleagues:

It is my pleasure to announce that [New Hire's Name] will be joining our company on [date] in the position of [Job Title]. We are excited to have [New Hire's Name], who joins us from [School or Company Name]. [He/She] is [preparing to take the CFP® Certification Exam/has passed the CFP® Certification Exam and is awaiting the work experience requirement/is a CFP® Professional] and brings a wealth of knowledge and is eager to serve you and contribute to our company. [New Hire's Name] will be working jointly with me to ensure that you receive the best possible service.

We're excited about [New Hire's Name] joining us, the growth of our company, and helping you achieve your life goals and dreams. Thank you for the trust and confidence that you've placed in us and for the referrals that you've been sending.

As always, feel free to contact us at [phone number] if you have any questions about your financial plan so that we can help guide you appropriately.

Sincerely,

[Your Name]

ACKNOWLEDGEMENTS

I want to thank Norm Boone for introducing me to Larry Ginsburg, and to Larry, Bryan Lee, Viktor Szucs, Bryan Clintsman, and others in the Dallas/Fort Worth FPA who took a chance on me as a young, unproven, new college graduate. I reflect on those early days of my career often and am truly overcome with gratitude. I also want to thank my mentors, friends, and colleagues that I have met thus far in my short journey in the financial planning profession. These relationships are dear to me. Michael Kitces, my business partner, who encouraged me to start writing regularly and for challenging me to keep it up even when I didn't think that I had much to say. Finally, thank you to my wife, Jenny, and children, Grace and Graylan, for motivating me, enduring my travel schedule, and loving me even when I have fallen short.

ABOUT THE AUTHOR

Caleb is the co-founder and CEO of New Planner Recruiting, a recruiting firm that specializes in sourcing, screening, and integrating financial planners in firms nationwide. He was named the Next Generation Influencer by *Financial Planning Magazine*, and one of the Top 25 Most Influential People in the Industry by *Investment Advisor Magazine*. In addition, Caleb was named to the prestigious 40 Under 40 list by *Investment News*.

As a graduate of Texas Tech University's Personal Financial Planning Program, Caleb has mentored, hired, managed, and coached thousands of career changers and college students seeking positions in financial planning, as well as the firm owners who hire them. For his outstanding accomplishments, he has been recognized as a Distinguished Alumnus for the Texas Tech University College of Human Sciences, as well as a Distinguished Alumnus for their Financial Planning Program.

Caleb is a Kolbe Certified™ Consultant, and original creator of the FPA Career Day program, which began with the Dallas/Fort Worth chapter and has subsequently been implemented by organizations across the country. He also serves as an adjunct faculty member for the University of Georgia's Financial Planning Program.

Outside of work, Caleb coaches boys' basketball for Downtown Ministries, a program designed to teach inner city youths necessary life skills. He is also an avid golfer, hiker, Tough Mudder, and snowboarder.

INDEX

Made in the USA
Columbia, SC
11 June 2018